Capital Punishment & Catholic Social Teaching: A Tradition of Support

By
David H. Lukenbill

A Chulu Press Book

Chulu Press First Edition published 2009

IBSN-13 978-0-9791670-7-2
IBSN-10 0-9791670-7-8

Published by The Lampstand Foundation

www.lampstandfoundation.org

For Marlene & Erika Always

——— ··· ———

The penitential criminal working to reform other criminals, wisely spends the rest of his life atoning for the harm he has done during his criminal life; not because the world requires it, but because the eternal balance requires it, his immortal soul requires it, and God wishes it.

Table of Contents

Foreword

This book is a defense of the scriptural and traditional Catholic position of support for capital punishment as expressed in the two universal catechisms, the *Catechism of the Council of Trent,* published by Pope Pius V in 1566, and the *Catechism of the Catholic Church,* published by Pope John Paul II in 1992 & 1997 (First & Second Edition), in response to calls for its abolition.

Based on scripture and tradition, calls for abolition are premature, though the call has generated a renewed focus on not only the magisterial history of this most ancient of teachings, but also its theological resonance within the expression of that teaching by the Fathers of the Church—ancient and modern—who most deeply reflected on it.

While Catholic social teaching has always supported capital punishment, it has been opposed by some in the Catholic hierarchy as an unnecessary criminal justice tool, with current criminal justice technology being presented as providing adequate protection of the innocent against the aggressor, meeting the criteria established by the Holy See (1997):

> **2267** Assuming that the guilty party's identity and responsibility have been fully determined, the traditional teaching of the Church does not exclude recourse to the death penalty, if this is the only possible way

of effectively defending human lives against the unjust aggressor.(Catechism # 2267)

Regarding the new restriction embedded in the traditional support, Flannery (2007) responds.

> It is true, of course, that traditional Catholic teaching does not exclude recourse to the death penalty; however, among traditional authors, it would be hard to find expressed the restriction, "when this is the only practicable way to defend lives of human beings effectively against the aggressor."
> (p. 414)

Though other examples of the inadequacy of current penal technology to protect the innocent will be noted later, it was dramatically witnessed in these recent cases reported by Witte (2009):

> Prisons around the nation are grappling with rising problems from prison inmates using cell phones to coordinate criminal activity. Officials are backing legislation to change the law to allow states to use cell phone jamming technology to render cell phones useless in prison.
>
> Texas State Sen. John Whitmire, whose life was threatened by a death row inmate with a cell phone, said cell phones smuggled inside prisons are the fastest growing and most alarming development in prison contraband

in Texas. He said corrections officials are in "a war" and need the jamming tool. ...

The dangerous and far-reaching aspects of prisoner cell phone use were illustrated in Maryland two years ago, when a Baltimore drug dealer used a cell phone to plan the killing of a witness from the city jail. In May, Patrick A. Byers Jr. was convicted of murdering Carl S. Lackl Jr., who had identified Byers as the gunman in a previous killing. (n.p.)

Capital punishment as a way of protecting the innocent is one of the central issues in the social teaching of the Church, but the ambiguity about it—particularly in the United States—over the past several decades after two millennia of certainty, places the credibility of the teaching itself at risk, and that negatively impacts the Church's social teaching as an effective tool for criminal transformation, further risking the immortal souls of those who are lost and whose being found largely relies on the constancy of the teaching of the Catholic Church, on eternally walking the eternal talking.

My personal thinking on capital punishment has gone through three phases.

As a former criminal—thief and robber—and having served twelve years in maximum security federal and state prisons where I gained an intimate knowledge of unrepentant evil, I was initially a supporter of capital punishment, especially for capital crimes against innocent women and children, crimes professional criminals always associate with its just use.

When I was becoming a Catholic, I moved in opposition to it, after being taught during the Rite of Christian Initiation for Adults (RCIA) that the Church was in opposition to it, and it was very important to me to think with the Church in all things.

After becoming Catholic and conducting my own study, I returned to a position of support when I learned that the Church's teaching did not oppose it, only the improper use of it. My position has become more certain as I realized how deeply support for capital punishment is woven into Church doctrine as an important aspect of the protection of the innocent against the murderer, "for all time" as the Holy See (1997) in the *Catechism* notes:

> **2260** The covenant between God and mankind is interwoven with reminders of God's gift of human life and man's murderous violence:
>
>> For your lifeblood I will surely require a reckoning.... Whoever sheds the blood of man, by man shall his blood be shed; for God made man in his own image. (Genesis 9:5-6)

The Old Testament always considered blood a sacred sign of life. (Leviticus 17:14) This teaching remains necessary for all time. (#2260)

John Paul II (1993) taught us the importance of the moral prescriptions of the Old Covenant:

> The moral prescriptions which God imparted in the Old Covenant, and which attained their perfection in the New and Eternal Covenant in the very person of the Son of God made man, must be *faithfully kept and continually put into practice* in the various different cultures throughout the course of history. The task of interpreting these prescriptions was entrusted by Jesus to the Apostles and to their successors, with the special assistance of the Spirit of truth: "He who hears you hears me" (*Lk* 10:16). By the light and the strength of this Spirit the Apostles carried out their mission of preaching the Gospel and of pointing out the "way" of the Lord (cf. *Acts* 18:25), teaching above all how to follow and imitate Christ: "For to me to live is Christ" (*Phil* 1:21). (#25)

The most important reason for writing about capital punishment is not to share my position of support, but to reaffirm the constancy of the teaching of the Church in the context of the general perception among many Catholics that the Church does oppose its use; an incorrect perception which needs to be addressed in relation to the transformation of criminals—which is the mission of my apostolate work with the Lampstand Foundation—of which constancy of doctrine is a core element of success.

One of the most important aspects in ensuring capital punishment remains an option for protecting the innocent is that it is a clear response to evil and it is vitally important that our Church remain committed to confronting and fighting evil directly; because ultimately, the constancy of the doctrine of the Church informs and animates its constancy in fighting evil and a central aspect of fighting evil is saving the souls of those imprisoned by it.

It is constancy that teaches and binds, it is the constancy of God, the Creator of Covenants; for what can the father of lies and a murderer from the beginning teach about constancy to truth.

There is also historical constancy among many of those who have opposed the Church most fervently about its support for capital punishment, such as the Waldenses, from the 12th century, noted by Weber (1912).

> They denounced all lying as a grievous sin, refused to take oaths and considered the shedding of human blood unlawful. They consequently condemned war and the infliction of the death penalty.

And the Albigenses from the 12th century, noted by Weber (1907).

> The dualism of the Albigenses was also the basis of their moral teaching...War and capital punishment were absolutely condemned.

And in modern times, the communist countries of the Soviet Bloc, noted by Glendon (2001) in her book about Eleanor Roosevelt, writing of the negotiations at the United Nations around the 1948 Universal Declaration of Human Rights:

> The Commission decided to retain the general statement "Everyone has the right to life, to liberty and security of person" rather than try to reach agreement on specific issues such as euthanasia, abortion, or the death penalty. This was a defeat for the representatives of Chile and Lebanon, who had pushed for express protection of the lives of the unborn, and for the Soviet-bloc delegates, who had argued for a ban on capital punishment. (p. 92)

Opposition to capital punishment has always been alive among certain thinkers within the Church, Tertullian and Lactantius among them, and two popes as noted by Stravinskas (1998):

> ...Popes Leo I (fifth century) and Nicholas I (ninth century) condemned the practice outright. (p. 192)

Part of the constancy of the social teaching on the efficacy of capital punishment as a function of the ancient and transcendent sword of justice, rests on its retributive purpose, about which Budziszewski (2004) notes:

> The question to ask about the retributive purpose of capital punishment is this: is it possible for punishment to signify the gravity of crimes which deserve death if their perpetuators are *never* visited with execution? This seems unlikely. Consider the deviant who tortures small children to death for his pleasure, or the ideologue who meditates the demise of innocent thousands for the sake of greater terror. Genesis says murderers deserve death *because* life is precious; man is made in the image of God. How convincing is our reverence for life if its mockers are suffered to live? (p. 116)

It is this reverence for life—in particular innocent life—that underlies the traditional support of the Catholic Church for the juridical use of capital punishment.

Introduction

The protection of life is the central animating core of the Catholic Church and while that principle is clearly understood in relation to the prohibition against abortion and euthanasia, it has, in our time, become confused in relation to the Church's support for Just War and the juridical use of capital punishment.

While support for capital punishment has always existed within the faithful of the Catholic Church (Newport, (2009) reports on Gallup Poll data that 61% of Catholics find capital punishment morally acceptable) we still encounter the damage done to the spiritual underpinning of Catholic social teaching connected with the responsibility to protect the innocent, by those opposing capital punishment, in the general confusion around the life issues it generates.

Pope John Paul II stated that if recourse to capital punishment is no longer necessary to protect the innocent—a huge *if* that does not yet exist—it may be abolished.

That papal support forms the foundation for the United States Conference of Catholic Bishops (USCCB) call to abolish capital punishment in the United States, and consequently, much of the intellectual and spiritual fuel for abolition comes from the USCCB work over many years, culminating in their 2005 Statement, *The Culture of Life and the Penalty of Death.*

An underlying argument—the "consistent ethic or seamless garment of life" approach—which many abolition advocates have used to conflate abortion, war, poverty, and euthanasia, with capital punishment, is seriously flawed.

A major problem with this argument—in addition that it is not congruent with the ancient teaching of the Church—is that it is innocent life that is protected by outlawing abortion and euthanasia, and innocent life that is also protected by supporting the juridical use of capital punishment and just war.

Abolishing capital punishment does not protect the life of the innocent, but may actually increase the danger.

The statements made by Pope John Paul II and supported by Pope Benedict XVI, who called upon all Catholics to approach capital punishment with extreme caution and care for the offender, remind us that *if* there are any means other than taking life, in which we can protect the life of the innocent from the aggressor, we should use them.

The most influential statement was made by Pope John Paul II (1999), where he said:

> The new evangelization calls for followers of Christ who are unconditionally pro-life: who will proclaim, celebrate and serve the Gospel of life in every situation. A sign of hope is the increasing recognition that the dignity of

human life must never be taken away, even in the case of someone who has done great evil. Modern society has the means of protecting itself, without definitively denying criminals the chance to reform (cf. *Evangelium Vitae*, 27). I renew the appeal I made most recently at Christmas for a consensus to end the death penalty, which is both cruel and unnecessary. (#5)

Regarding "society has the means of protecting itself", the situation in the United States where our legal system guarantees right of visitation and communication in even the most secure confinement—as in a super-max prison or on death row, the aggressor still has the capacity to reach out and harm the innocent, whether through the possession of contraband cell phones, information transmitted through attorneys, guards, and visitors—and it is in this context that criminal justice professionals require the continued option of capital punishment; and it is from this perspective of still being able to threaten the innocent, that the magisterium of the Catholic Church, expressed through the centuries, continues to support capital punishment, as stated by the Holy See (1997)

> **2267** The traditional teaching of the Church does not exclude, presupposing full ascertainment of the identity and responsibility of the offender, recourse to the death penalty, when this is the only

practicable way to defend the lives of human beings effectively against the aggressor.

If, instead, bloodless means are sufficient to defend against the aggressor and to protect the safety of persons, public authority should limit itself to such means, because they better correspond to the concrete conditions of the common good and are more in conformity to the dignity of the human person.

Today, in fact, given the means at the State's disposal to effectively repress crime by rendering inoffensive the one who has committed it, without depriving him definitively of the possibility of redeeming himself, cases of absolute necessity for suppression of the offender 'today … are very rare, if not practically non-existent.' (Catechism #2267)

A note on the already "very rare" use of the death penalty from the Bureau of Justice Statistics (2006) from the period of 2000 to 2006 there were 114,302 murders and non-negligent manslaughters in the United States and during that same period there were 459 executions, for an execution rate of 0.40%, "very rare" by any definition. (n.p)

If the system of confinement in the United States can advance to the point where the aggressor is confined so completely that communication is blocked by any means with the outside world, through outside contact by contraband cell phones, through guards, family, priests, or attorneys—all capable of being innocently manipulated or co-opted—and if the possibility of a future legislative change of current lifetime sentences resulting in release, then a truly bloodless means of protecting the innocent from the aggressor might have been reached and abolition can perhaps be then fruitfully discussed.

Capital punishment is essentially a theological issue and an eminent American theologian, Avery Cardinal Dulles (2004) made an important point regarding reversing the traditional support of the Church for capital punishment:

> The reversal of a doctrine as well established as the legitimacy of capital punishment would raise serious problems regarding the credibility of the magisterium. Consistency with scripture and long-standing Catholic tradition is important for the grounding of many current teachings of the Catholic Church; for example, those regarding abortion, contraception, the permanence of marriage, and the ineligibility of women for priestly ordination. If the tradition on capital punishment had been reversed, serious questions would be raised regarding other doctrines.... (p. 26)

It is only within theology that evil—the deepest dimension of crime—can be addressed. It is evil which must concern us in addressing crime, and we must recognize that evil rarely reforms, but most criminals can and will, given a reason and shown the way, as St Thomas Aquinas (1920) taught:

> When, however, they fall into very great wickedness, and become incurable, we ought no longer to show them friendliness. It is for this reason that both Divine and human laws command such like sinners to be put to death, because there is greater likelihood of their harming others than of their mending their ways. Nevertheless the judge puts this into effect, not out of hatred for the sinners, but out of the love of charity, by reason of which he prefers the public good to the life of the individual. Moreover the death inflicted by the judge profits the sinner, if he be converted, unto the expiation of his crime; and, if he be not converted, it profits so as to put an end to the sin, because the sinner is thus deprived of the power to sin any more." (Ques. 25, Article 6, reply to objection 2.)

The most powerful example of "the death inflicted by the judge profits the sinner" is that of Dismas, The Good Thief, who established the eternal model of the efficacy of capital punishment to call forth deep and true penance, which Christ, in the open confessional of Golgotha, rendered forgiveness and elevation to sainthood.

Capital Punishment & Matthew 18:6

Catholic social teaching helps us understand that capital punishment is the only sanction potent enough to create the redemptive environment most apt to influence the deeply evil sinner and that temporal death is much to be preferred over an eternal torment in hell.

$\mathfrak{M}$atthew 18:6 "Whoever causes one of these little ones who believe in me to sin, it would be better for him to have a great millstone hung around his neck and to be drowned in the depths of the sea." Is perhaps the clearest expression of support for capital punishment spoken by Christ, as Amerio (1996) notes:

> In the Gospel, Christ indirectly sanctions capital punishment when he says it would be better for a man to be condemned to death by drowning than to commit the sin of scandal. (p. 432)

The Catholic & Protestant commentaries about this verse and the teaching of the entire chapter reveal the vigorous sanctions—capital punishment and banishment—Christ taught as applying to the members of the Church community who violate its teachings. Matthew 18 has long been acknowledged as a *Discourse on the Church*, but not enough Catholic attention has been devoted to its support for capital punishment.

The necessary horizon and knowledge for understanding capital punishment as expressed in Matthew 18:6 is eternity and hell respectively.

Christ teaches his disciples that the eternal torment of hell awaits the tempter who, through scandal, cause the converted believers in him to sin, and the Holy See (1997) notes: "he may even draw his brother into spiritual death" (Catechism #2284), and it is better for the tempter that he be put to death, in the hope that facing temporal death, he will seek redemption and mercy from God and perhaps be saved from eternal torment.

The importance of examining Matthew 18:6 in relation to capital punishment is twofold; Matthew 18's status as a discourse on the Church and its support for capital punishment in Christ's own words—a powerful affirmation of the responsibility of the community to protect the innocent and save the sinner.

The perspective from the field of modern historico-critical biblical scholarship often looks at Matthew 18:6 as an example of hyperbole, an analysis which often causes confusion about the truth Christ spoke. Pope Benedict XVI has spoken of the generally corrosive effect of some historico-critical interpretation:

> The rule of faith, yesterday as today, is not based on the discoveries (be they true or hypothetical) of biblical sources and layers but on the Bible *just as it is,* as it has been

read in the Church since the time of the Fathers until now. It is precisely the fidelity to this reading of the Bible that has given us the saints; who were often uneducated and, at any rate, frequently knew nothing about exegetical contexts. Yet they were the ones who understood it best. (Ratzinger, 1985, p. 76)

More recently, Pope Benedict XVI (2009) has spoken of the three foundations which we must use to interpret scripture text correctly, as noted by Magister (2009):

> What this means is that one must: 1) interpret the text while taking into account the unity of all of Scripture; today, this is called canonical exegesis; at the time of the council, this term had not yet been created, but the council says the same thing: the unity of all of Scripture must be taken into account; 2) one must also keep in mind the living tradition of the entire Church, and finally 3) one must observe the harmony that exists between elements of the faith.

Reflecting on Matthew 18:6 through the three interpretive tools offered: scriptural unity, Church tradition, and harmony, does reveal that Christ was speaking of capital punishment.

The Old Testament spoke at length about capital punishment and many sinful activities were determined to justify bringing the sanction down upon the individual. The New Testament has not been as rich in instruction around this harshest of punishments, and modern Catholic commentaries connecting Matthew 18:6 to a supportive position for capital punishment are rare, so we now must look to those from tradition for support.

Commentary

This is helpful commentary by Haydock (1859) of Matthew 18:6:

> **Ver. 6.** By these strong expressions of our Lord, we may judge of the enormity and malice of scandal. Rather than be the cause of scandal to any of the faithful, and occasion the loss of his soul, we must be ready to undergo every torment, yes, and suffer death itself. (Denis the Carthusian) --- The ancient punishment among the Greeks for sacrilege was drowning, with a mill-stone fastened about the neck, according to Diodorus Siculus. (n.p.)

Christ thus clearly states in Matthew 18:6 the justified fate of those tempters who would kill the souls of those new to Christ.

The Protestant Matthew Henry (1706) comments on Matthew 18:6:

> The punishment of this crime; intimated in that word, *Better for him that he were*

drowned in the depth of the sea. The sin is so heinous, and the ruin proportionally so great, that he had better undergo the sorest punishments inflicted on the worst of malefactors, which can only kill the body. Hell is worse than the depth of the sea; for it is a bottomless pit, and it is a burning lake. The depth of the sea is only killing, but hell is tormenting. (n.p.)

Matthew 18 is called the discourse on the Church as noted by Navarre (1988):

[1-35] The teachings of Jesus recorded in chapter 18 of St. Matthew are often called the "discourse on the Church" or "ecclesiastical discourse" because they are a series of instruction on the way in which his Church is to be administered. ..

In vv. 6-10 Jesus emphasizes the fatherly care which pastors of the Church should have for the "little ones"—a term which covers everyone in need of special care for whatever reason (because they are recent converts, or are not well grounded in Church teaching, or are not yet adults, etc.) ...

Thus, the whole of chapter 18, the "discourse on the Church", is a survey of the future history of the Church during its earthly stage, and a series of practical rules of conduct for Christians—a kind of compliment to the Sermon on the Mount, (chapters 5-7), which is a "magna carta" for the new Kingdom established by Christ. (pp. 160-161)

The responsibility that the community has to protect the innocent has long been a core principle of the Catholic Church and it was also a central aspect of the 1948 *United Nations Declaration of Human Rights,* heavily influenced by Catholic thought, and the United Nations Report (2001), *The Responsibility to Protect,* which stated as two basic principles:

> A. State sovereignty implies responsibility, and the primary responsibility for the protection of its people lies with the state itself.

> B. Where a population is suffering serious harm, as a result of internal war, insurgency, repression or state failure, and the state in question is unwilling or unable to halt or avert it, the principle of non-intervention yields to the international responsibility to protect. (p. xi)

Pope Benedict XVI (2008) addressed the responsibility to protect in his talk to the United Nations:

> Recognition of the unity of the human family, and attention to the innate dignity of every man and woman, today find renewed emphasis in the principle of the

28

responsibility to protect. This has only recently been defined, but it was already present implicitly at the origins of the United Nations, and is now increasingly characteristic of its activity. Every State has the primary duty to protect its own population from grave and sustained violations of human rights, as well as from the consequences of humanitarian crises, whether natural or man-made. If States are unable to guarantee such protection, the international community must intervene with the juridical means provided in the United Nations Charter and in other international instruments. (n.p.)

The responsibility to protect the innocent also animates the acceptance of Just War and the disapproval of abortion and euthanasia—foundational protection of life pillars of the Church—ancient and modern.

Jesus speaks clearly when condemning those who would scandalize those who believe in him—by tempting and leading them to sin—to suffer the ancient form of capital punishment used by the Greeks, "drowning, with a mill-stone fastened about the neck".

The Holy See (1997) teaches:

> **2284** Scandal is an attitude or behavior which leads another to do evil. The person who gives scandal becomes his neighbor's

tempter. He damages virtue and integrity; he may even draw his brother into spiritual death. Scandal is a grave offense if by deed or omission another is deliberately led into a grave offense.

2285 Scandal takes on a particular gravity by reason of the authority of those who cause it or the weakness of those who are scandalized.... Scandal is grave when given by those who by nature or office are obliged to teach and educate others. Jesus reproaches the scribes and Pharisees on this account: he likens them to wolves in sheep's clothing. (Catechism 2284-2285)

With that method of capital punishment prescribed, attempting to proscribe it, as many in the Church are attempting to do, appears deeply incongruent; in addition to disregarding the possibility of the spur of temporal death leading to redemptive liberation from eternal torment.

We cannot forget we have eternal life, and it is the spur of eternity that often brings redemption to an evil soul facing the certainty of temporal death. That is the good, the charity, that St. Thomas Aquinas and the magisterium of the Church, speaks of in relation to its strong and ancient support of capital punishment.

Change

The recent change by some leaders within the Catholic Church about capital punishment is examined by Amerio (1996):

> An important change has occurred in the Church regarding the theology of punishment. We could cite the French bishops' document that asserted in 1979 that the death penalty ought to be abolished in France as it was *incompatible with the Gospel*, the Canadian and American bishop's statements on the matter, and the articles in the *Ossevatore Romano* calling for the abolition of the death penalty, as injurious to human dignity and contrary to the Gospel.

> ...one cannot cancel out the Old Testament's decrees regarding the death penalty, by a mere stroke of the pen. Nor can canon law, still less the teaching of the New Testament, be canceled out at a stroke. I am well aware that the famous passage in Romans (Rm 13:4) giving princes the *ius gladii* (the right use of the sword), and calling them the ministers of God to punish the wicked, has been emptied of meaning by the canons of the new hermeneutic, on the grounds that it is the product of a past set of historical circumstances. Pius XII however explicitly rejected that view, in a speech to Catholic jurists on 5 February 1955, and said that the passage of St. Paul was of permanent and

31

universal value, because it refers to the essential foundation of penal authority and to its inherent purpose. (p. 432)

There was also a change in the wording on capital punishment in sections 2266-2267, of the first edition of the *Catechism of the Catholic Church*, published by the Holy See (1992), which said:

Legitimate Defense

2266 Preserving the common good of society requires rendering the aggressor unable to inflict harm. For this reason, the traditional teaching of the Church has acknowledged as well-founded the right and duty of legitimate public authority to punish malefactors by means of penalties commensurate with the gravity of the crime not excluding, in cases of extreme gravity, the death penalty. For analogous reasons those holding authority have the right to repel by armed force aggressors against the community in their charge.

The primary effect of *punishment* is to redress the disorder caused by the offense. When his punishment is voluntarily accepted by the offender, it takes on the value of expiation. Moreover, punishment has the effect of preserving public order and the safety of persons. Finally punishment has a medicinal value; as far as possible it should contribute to the correction of the offender.

2267 If bloodless means are sufficient to defend human lives against an aggressor and to protect public order and the safety of persons, public authority should limit itself to such means, because they better correspond to the concrete conditions of the common good and are more in conformity to the dignity of the human person. (Catechism #2266-2267)

and that of the second edition, published by the Holy See (1997), which says:

Capital Punishment

2266 The State's effort to contain the spread of behaviors injurious to human rights and the fundamental rules of civil coexistence corresponds to the requirement of watching over the common good. Legitimate public authority has the right and duty to inflict penalties commensurate with the gravity of the crime. The primary scope of the penalty is to redress the disorder caused by the offense. When his punishment is voluntarily accepted by the offender, it takes on the value of expiation. Moreover, punishment, in addition to preserving public order and the safety of persons, has a medicinal scope: as far as possible it should contribute to the correction of the offender.

2267 The traditional teaching of the Church does not exclude, presupposing full ascertainment of the identity and responsibility of the offender, recourse to the death penalty, when this is the only practicable way to defend the lives of human beings effectively against the aggressor.

If, instead, bloodless means are sufficient to defend against the aggressor and to protect the safety of persons, public authority should limit itself to such means, because they better correspond to the concrete conditions of the common good and are more in conformity to the dignity of the human person.

Today, in fact, given the means at the State's disposal to effectively repress crime by rendering inoffensive the one who has committed it, without depriving him definitively of the possibility of redeeming himself, cases of absolute necessity for suppression of the offender 'today ... are very rare, if not practically non-existent.' (Catechism #2266-2267)

From the first edition of 1992 to the second edition of 1997—five short years—the *Catechism*, the magisterial heart of the Church, moves from clear support by affirmation to muddy support by deprecation.

This is a significant movement and one wonders what led to this change.

We know that the new and more restrictive language on the use of capital punishment in the second edition originated from the encyclical of Pope John Paul II, *Evangelium Vitae,* of March 25, 1995, and for an explanation of the change in language, we have the words of Joseph Cardinal Ratzinger (Pope Benedict XVI) who presided over the Interdicasterial Commission for the *Catechism of the Catholic Church*, responsible for overseeing the publication of the Second Edition of the *Catechism,* reported by Neuhaus (1995):

> Clearly, the Holy Father [John Paul II] has not altered the doctrinal principles which pertain to this issue as they are presented in the Catechism, but has simply deepened the application of such principles in the context of present-day historical circumstances. Thus, where other means for the self-defense of society are possible and adequate, the death penalty may be permitted to disappear. (n.p.)

While the change in language in the Catechism emanating from *Evangelium Vitae* may be beneficial for modern ears, it is not necessarily so for those reductionists assuming it signifies a true doctrinal change in the traditional support of capital punishment, a notion challenged by Long (1999).

The Magisterial judgment of *Evangelium vitae* concerning the legitimacy of capital punishment constitutes—as emphasized anew by its insertion within *The Catechism of the Catholic Church*—the most important modern locus for understanding the Church's teaching on this topic. The position presented in this encyclical has figured prominently in more recent papal and episcopal statements dealing with the death penalty. The question that has created some confusion is what kind of teaching is being presented. A common interpretation is that *Evangelium vitae* marks a doctrinal development: the encyclical is said to restrict use of the death penalty to cases where it is absolutely necessary for the physical protection of society in a sense comparable to the use of lethal force in self-defense.

Yet such a reading neglects numerous and substantial contributions from the tradition that argue for a different understanding of the penalty's legitimacy. It is the nearly unanimous opinion of the Fathers and Doctors of the Church that the death penalty is morally licit, and the teaching of past popes (and numerous catechisms) that this penalty is essentially just (and even that its validity is not subject to cultural variation) (p. 511)

After an extensive refutation of the reductionist argument, Long concludes:

From a Thomistic vantage point, the reductionist interpretation of *Evangelium vitae* is difficult to reconcile with Catholic tradition, because this tradition must consider the political state as providentially bound to acknowledge and implement a morally transcendent order of justice. So long as Catholics do not become contract theorists or Hobbesians, they must conceive the state as executing an order of justice that transcends it in origin, majesty, and truth. Only on such a ground does punishment as a righting of moral imbalance make sense. (p.548)

So, while what was changed was a more sensitive appreciation of the seriousness of capital punishment and an expression of a sincere hope that someday, in some way, under some conditions, it may not be necessary to resort to capital punishment, that time is not here yet, not yet.

The preparation of both editions of the *Catechism* was a lengthy one.

Weigel (1999) comments on the first edition:

The *Catechism* went through nine drafts, all of which were first prepared in French. Bishops around the world were consulted throughout the drafting process, and the editorial committee's work was continually reviewed by the oversight commission [chaired by Cardinal Joseph Ratzinger, now

Pope Benedict XVI] John Paul followed the work closely, according to Schonborn, but rarely gave direct comments on the draft. One exception, widely noted, was the catechism's discussion of the morality of capital punishment... (p. 661)

Weigel (1999) also notes Pope John Paul II's reference to capital punishment in the encyclical *Evangelium Vitae*:

> The striking development in *Evangelium Vitae* was on capital punishment. The Church's tradition, based on the Bible, had defended capital punishment not only in terms of societal self-defense but as just retribution for an evil done and as a deterrent against future crime. The *Catechism of the Catholic Church* had reviewed this classic reasoning while seeming to narrow the scope of the death penalty's justification to societal self-defense: if nonleathal means were available to protect society from an aggressor, they ought to be used. Now, John Paul narrowed the criterion of social self-defense in cases of "absolute necessity", even further, suggesting that "today...as a result of steady improvements in the organization of the penal system, such cases are very rare, if not practically non-existent." The *Catechism* was subsequently revised in its definitive Latin edition to cohere with the encyclical's teaching, which seemed to reflect Karol

Wojtyla's experience of, and loathing for, the state's power of execution. It was an issue on which the Pope had strong personal feelings, but it had not matured to the point where the consensus that had been cited in *Evangelium Vitae's* teaching on abortion and euthanasia could be invoked. The encyclical's silence about the traditional arguments from retributive justice and deterrence seemed likely to fuel further debate on the issue. (p. 758)

The fourth reason for capital punishment from Catholic teaching—not mentioned by Weigel—is that it is the only sanction potent enough to create the redemptive environment for the deeply evil sinner, within which he may seek the forgiveness of God, forgiveness that will come when truly sought, as St. Thomas Aquinas, (1920) the Angelic Doctor of the Church notes:

> According to the order of His wisdom, God sometimes slays sinners forthwith in order to deliver the good, whereas sometimes He allows them time to repent, according as He knows what is expedient for His elect. This also does human justice imitate according to its powers; for it puts to death those who are dangerous to others, while it allows time for repentance to those who sin without grievously harming others. (Ques. 64 Article 2, reply to objection 2.)

Avery Cardinal Dulles (2004) comments on the fourth reason:

> 4. *Rehabilitation*. Although execution does not of course reintegrate offenders into society, it prevents hardened criminals from spiritually harming themselves by further sin. The prospect of imminent execution is a powerful inducement to repentance and reconciliation with God, as many accounts of ministry to convicts on death row attest. (p. 24)

John Paul II's expression of an appeal to reach a consensus on ending the use of the death penalty: "I renew the appeal I made most recently at Christmas for a consensus to end the death penalty, which is both cruel and unnecessary." (St. Louis homily, January 1999)—though not so strongly felt as to result in inclusion in the Catechism, was deeply felt, and possibly grew, in addition to his historical revulsion at the state's use of violence, from his long struggle against a central dissent of his papacy, liberation theology and the violence often arising from it.

In battling liberation theology adherents—some of whom were priests—who felt justified in taking up arms to help liberate the poor from oppression in Latin America; John Paul answered, as Weigel (1999) notes:

> He [John Paul II] did insist that authentic liberation from totalitarianism could not

adopt totalitarianism's violent instruments if it were to remain true to its purpose. (p. 440)

It is a very short step from this to feeling that the violence of capital punishment—in the supposedly secure imprisonment environment of the super-max prison in America—was no longer morally acceptable to protect innocent life, as noted by the USCCB (2005):

> State-sanctioned killing in our names diminishes all of us. (p. 3)

The problem with this leap—if that played any role in the change—beyond the violence it does to millennia of Church teaching, is that super-max confinement does not protect the innocent from the aggressor in an American context, and numerous instances of criminal enterprises—often involving the ordering of death for the innocent witnesses of crimes as already noted—are commonly known by correctional and prosecutorial professionals.

The second edition of the *Catechism*, however, due to this newer language, has proven to be more congruent with the USCCB call to change the ancient teaching than the first edition, as the clarity of capital punishment support—while still evident in the second edition—can be interpreted as not being quite as supportive and suggesting a case for abolition, as many researchers and bishops have chosen to do.

A judgment about this comes from Supreme Court Justice, Antonin Scalia (2002):

> I am therefore happy to learn from the canonical experts I have consulted that the position set forth in *Evangelium Vitae* and in the latest version of the Catholic catechism does not purport to be binding teaching—that is, it need not be accepted by practicing Catholics, though they must give it thoughtful and respectful consideration. It would be remarkable to think otherwise—that a couple of paragraphs in an encyclical almost entirely devoted not to crime and punishment but to abortion and euthanasia was intended authoritatively to sweep aside (if one could) two thousand years of Christian teaching. (n.p.)

It is clear that the second edition of the *Catechism*, while retaining the traditional support of capital punishment, embraces its current rarity (US execution rate of 0.40%) and anticipates a future level of carceral development—though super-max prisons in America were hoped to be that development, it has not yet proven to be so—where the evil aggressor can be restrained from harming the innocent.

There may indeed come a time when the security of prison for life is so powerfully punitive and secluded from being able to harm the innocent, that expiation may occur and, within that deep solitude, the aggressor may seek redemption.

Conclusion

In Matthew 18, Christ is teaching the apostles about how to deal with the deep sinners in the new Church that will arise after he is gone and that they must be prepared to cut people off if they are not willing to repent, but he is clear in verse 6, that there are some sins, those of scandal, that are so serious that even the ultimate punishment may be required.

Christ universalized the Torah, as Pope Benedict XVI teaches:

> Jesus' universalization of the Torah, as the New Testament understands it, is not the extraction of a few universal moral prescriptions from the living totality of the revelation of God. This universalization retains the unity of cult and ethics. Ethics remains grounded and anchored in the worship of God. (Ratzinger, 1997, p. 92)

This universalization brought many of the Old Testament capital punishment prescriptions within the umbrella of the New Testament's law of scandal as much of the Decalogue was brought into the embrace of the Great Commandment.

Historic Catholic support for capital punishment— as part of the long tradition protecting the innocent—is vital to the social teaching of the Church, as that teaching needs to remain true to itself if it is to retain its potency in the conversion and transformation of criminals, and all other sinners.

To overturn a principle as ancient as the judicial use of capital punishment, could bring all of its enduring principles into question.

The USCCB is calling for this and the Holy Father has remarked on the teaching authority status of the episcopal conference:

> The decisive new emphasis on the role of the bishops is in reality restrained or actually risks being smothered by the insertion of bishops into episcopal conferences that are ever more organized, often with burdensome bureaucratic structures. We must not forget that the episcopal conferences have no theological basis, they do not belong to the structure of the Church, as willed by Christ, that cannot be eliminated; they have only a practical, concrete function. No episcopal conference, as such, has a teaching mission; its documents have no weight of their own save that of the consent given by the individual bishops.
>
> It is a matter of safeguarding the very nature of the Catholic Church, which is based on an episcopal structure and not on a kind of federation of national churches. The national level is not an ecclesial dimension. (Ratzinger, 1985, pp. 59-60)

Archbishop Donald W. Wuerl (2008) appears to agree:

> I have always respected the role of the local Church and the ministry of the individual bishop as shepherd of the Church entrusted to his care. For that reason, I have not accepted the suggestions that the Archdiocese of Washington or episcopal conferences have some particular role that supersedes the authority of an individual bishop in his particular Church. (n.p)

David Hollenbach, (2008) S.J., Director of the Center for Human Rights and International Justice, is a little harsher—deservedly so—in his comments on the status of the credibility of the teaching authority of the bishops of the United States:

> Sad to say, the U.S. bishops have, in my judgment, lost much of their credibility in the domains of social justice and peace in the past few years. This is due, in large part, to the scandal of clerical sexual abuse and the way a number of bishops responded to it, including the bishop in the city where I live, Boston. It is hard to imagine a more blatant violation of justice than the sexual abuse of young people. The fact that this has been done by priests and that some bishops have tried to cover it up threatens to make all talk of the church's mission of justice sound like gross hypocrisy.

In addition, a small number of U.S. bishops have recently so stressed a narrow set of moral issues related to sexuality in their engagement with political life that they have threatened to overshadow other initiatives of church leaders in the domain of social justice and peace. Both the sexual abuse crisis and the issue of single-issue intervention in the political sphere raise very basic questions about the governance of Catholic Church today. (p. 321)

Matthew 18:6 is also considered directed at evil priests, as Gregory the Great notes:

> **1102** ... Hence also it is written through the prophet, *A snare for the downfall of my people are evil priests (Os 5,1 Os 9,8)*. Hence again the Lord through the prophet says of the priests, *They are made to be for a stumbling-block of iniquity to the house of Israel.* For certainly no one does more harm in the Church than one who has the name and rank of sanctity, while he acts perversely. For him, when he transgresses, no one presumes to take to task; and the offence spreads forcibly for example, when out of reverence to his rank the sinner is honoured. But all who are unworthy would fly from the burden of so great guilt, if with the attentive ear of the heart they weighed the sentence of the Truth, *Whoso shall offend one of these little ones which believe in me, it were better for him that a millstone*

were hanged about his neck, and he were drowned in the depth of the sea (*Mt 18, 6*). By the millstone is expressed the round and labour of worldly life, and by the depth of the sea is denoted final damnation. Whosoever, then, having come to bear the outward show of sanctity, either by word or example destroys others, it had indeed been better for him that earthly deeds in open guise should press him down to death than that sacred offices should point him out to others as imitable in his wrong-doing; because, surely, if he fell alone, the pains of hell would torment him in more tolerable degree. (n.p.)

Today, the Church's social teaching protects the innocent from four major aggressors; the abortionist, the terrorist, the sexual predator, and the criminal, and against each its teaching must be steadfast and true, for it is a light unto the world.

Catholic Social Teaching & Capital Punishment

"Another kind of lawful slaying belongs to the civil authorities, to whom is entrusted power of life and death, by the legal and judicious exercise of which they punish the guilty and protect the innocent. The just use of this power, far from involving the crime of murder, is an act of paramount obedience to this Commandment, which prohibits murder. The end of the Commandment is the preservation and security of human life."
(Roman Catechism, p. 421)

What the Catechism says of the statements from Christ concerning capital punishment in Matthew 18:6, Holy See (1997):

> **2285** Scandal takes on a particular gravity by reason of the authority of those who cause it or the weakness of those who are scandalized. It prompted our Lord to utter this curse: "Whoever causes one of these little ones who believe in me to sin, it would be better for him to have a great millstone fastened round his neck and to be drowned in the depth of the sea."[85] [Mt 18:6; Cf. ,1 Cor 8:10-13] Scandal is grave when given by those who by nature or office are obliged to teach and educate others. Jesus reproaches the scribes and Pharisees on this account: he likens them to wolves in sheep's clothing.[86] [Cf. Mt 7:15.]

And the explanatory notes about Matthew 18:6 from the University of Navarre (1988):

The holy, pained indignation sounding in Jesus' words show the seriousness of the sin of scandal, which is defined as something said, done or omitted which leads another person to commit sin"

> "Millstone": our Lord is referring to a form of [capital] punishment used in ancient times which consisted in throwing a person into the sea with a heavy weight attached to his neck to prevent his body floating to the surface; this was regarded as a particularly ignominious form of death because it was inflicted only on the worst criminals and also because it meant deprival of burial.

> Although Jesus affirms that people will cause others to sin, this does not mean that everyone, personally, should not ensure that this does not happen. Therefore, everyone who does cause another to sin is responsible for his action. Here he refers directly to scandal given to children—an action that is particularly malicious given the weakness and innocence of children. (p. 162)

Saint Augustine (426 A.D., 1991 edition) addressed capital punishment:

> The same divine authority that forbids the killing of a human being establishes certain exceptions, as when God authorizes killing

by a general law or when He gives an explicit commission to an individual for a limited time. The agent who executes the killing does not commit homicide; he is an instrument as is the sword with which he cuts. Therefore, it is in no way contrary to the commandment, 'Thou shalt not kill' to wage war at God's bidding, or for the representatives of public authority to put criminals to death, according to the law, that is, the will of the most just reason. (p. 27)

The *Roman Catechism* (1982) The Catechism of the Council of Trent (1545-1563) stated:

Execution of Criminals

Another kind of lawful slaying belongs to the civil authorities, to whom is entrusted power of life and death, by the legal and judicious exercise of which they punish the guilty and protect the innocent. The just use of this power, far from involving the crime of murder, is an act of paramount obedience to this Commandment which prohibits murder. The end of the Commandment is the preservation and security of human life. Now the punishments inflicted by the civil authority, which is the legitimate avenger of crime, naturally tend to this end, since they give security to life by repressing outrage and violence. Hence these words of David: In the morning I put to death all the wicked of the land, that I might cut off all the workers of iniquity from the city of the Lord. (p. 421) (*St Pius X Catechism, 417*)

This clear historic approval is validated by Willis (1911):

> Canon law has always forbidden clerics to shed human blood and therefore capital punishment has always been the work of the officials of the State and not of the Church. Even in the case of heresy, of which so much is made by non-Catholic controversialists, the functions of ecclesiastics were restricted invariably to ascertaining the fact of heresy. The punishment, whether capital or other, was both prescribed and inflicted by civil government. The infliction of capital punishment is not contrary to the teaching of the Catholic Church, and the power of the State to visit upon culprits the penalty of death derives much authority from revelation and from the writings of theologians. The advisability of exercising that power is, of course, an affair to be determined upon other and various considerations. (n.p.)

Capital punishment is a rooted part of the Church's long advocated protection of the innocent against the aggressor, whether through the abortion and euthanasia prohibition or the Just War principles.

The recent call for an end to the use of capital punishment when other means can be used to protect the innocent from the aggressor, has been built on a underexplored reference to the Catholic historic record regarding criminal justice issues; and the current understanding among criminal justice professionals that even within the confines of a maximum security prison, criminals are still able to influence aggression against the innocent.

To show the emerging attempt at changing the past approval, from Stravinskas (1998):

> Capital punishment, often in barbaric and horrendous forms, existed in all of the ancient law codes, including that of the Old Testament Jews. With the coming of Christianity, the appropriateness of capital punishment was taken up by Christian leaders and teachers.
>
> Tertullian, Lactantius and Popes Leo 1 (fifth century) and Nicholas (ninth century) condemned the practice outright. St. Augustine, although he did not condemn it, called for mercy in dealing with accused criminals.
>
> The Church has never officially condemned capital punishment. When asked for the Catholic opinion on the issue, reference is often made to St. Thomas Aquinas, who approved of capital punishment for the good of the community and upheld the right of legitimate government to take the life of a criminal guilty of a serious crime. (p. 192)

An even greater handicap in presenting a proper analysis of criminal justice is the modern tendency to discount and properly understand the hard reality of the deep involvement of Satan in the criminal world, and could it be any more obvious, that within the darkest bowels of our nation's maximum security prisons, the animating visage is surely his; a fact known by all those living within the steel and stone.

Too many who study criminal justice issues fail to face Satan and his works and too often excuse crime as a result of structural sin, and become apologists for criminal behavior, rather than realizing it for what it often is, the work of the devil; and thus does he continue his greatest deception, of continuing the lie that he does not even exist.

As the Holy See (1997) teaches us:

> **2850** The last petition to our Father is also included in Jesus' prayer: "I am not asking you to take them out of the world, but I ask you to protect them from the evil one." It touches each of us personally, but it is always "we" who pray, in communion with the whole Church, for the deliverance of the whole human family. The Lord's Prayer continually opens us to the range of God's economy of salvation. Our interdependence in the drama of sin and death is turned into solidarity in the Body of Christ, the "communion of saints."

2851 In this petition, evil is not an abstraction, but refers to a person, Satan, the Evil One, the angel who opposes God. The devil (dia-bolos) is the one who "throws himself across" God's plan and his work of salvation accomplished in Christ. (Catechism # 2850-2851)

Those working within the social science field, informed by Catholic teaching and with a professional knowledge of criminal justice issues and a deeper understanding of the hand of Satan within the criminal world, are in support of the teaching, as noted by Rice (2007) that:

> Even under John Paul's teaching one could still argue for the death penalty in some cases, for example, if a life inmate, already in maximum security, murders another inmate, or where the state is unable to confine inmates securely...
>
> It might be argued that even John Paul's criteria could justify execution of a terrorist leader if his continued existence in prison would incite further terrorist attacks. (Volume 1, p. 283)

The Church's traditional support for capital punishment—validated in Catholic teaching for millennia—is based on the assumption of the reality of evil (which the relativist thinking secular world, clearly influencing the Church in the West, struggles to accept), that some offenses are so terrible that the only just and charitable response is to consign the evildoer to hell, and hope that within that definite period of earthly life he now knows remains to him after sentenced to death , he will be spurred to seek forgiveness.

The Catholic Catechism (TCC) Hardon (1981) notes:

> Capital punishment is part of the acknowledged Christian tradition... (p. 345)

The TCC was considered authoritative by Siegmund (2007), who noted:

> [It] was not really surpassed as the standard in the United States until the magisterium itself promulgated the *Catechism of the Catholic Church.* (p. 494)

Dulles (2001) gives us a good historical overview of opinions around the development of the doctrine of capital punishment during the relatively modern period:

> In modern times Doctors of the Church such as Robert Bellarmine and Alphonsus Liguori held that certain criminals should be punished by death. Venerable authorities such as Francisco de Vitoria, Thomas More, and Francisco Suárez agreed. John Henry Newman, in a letter to a friend, maintained that the magistrate had the right to bear the sword, and that the Church should sanction

its use, in the sense that Moses, Joshua, and Samuel used it against abominable crimes.

Throughout the first half of the twentieth century the consensus of Catholic theologians in favor of capital punishment in extreme cases remained solid, as may be seen from approved textbooks and encyclopedia articles of the day. The Vatican City State from 1929 until 1969 had a penal code that included the death penalty for anyone who might attempt to assassinate the pope. Pope Pius XII, in an important allocution to medical experts, declared that it was reserved to the public power to deprive the condemned of the benefit of life in expiation of their crimes.

Summarizing the verdict of Scripture and tradition, we can glean some settled points of doctrine. It is agreed that crime deserves punishment in this life and not only in the next. In addition, it is agreed that the State has authority to administer appropriate punishment to those judged guilty of crimes and that this punishment may, in serious cases, include the sentence of death. (n.p.)

The proper response to evil is punishment—appropriately found in Hell—and capital punishment speeds that consequence while human mercy delays God's judgment, so clearly stated by Christ with the millstone statement in Matthew 18:6.

During the period of the 1960's through the 1980's certain religious orders, cardinals, bishops, and parish priests of the Catholic Church—particularly in the Americas—became enamored of the Marxist-inspired liberation theology, and informed by its anti-capitalism, absorbed the corresponding attributes of restricting the religious, economic, legal, and military power of capitalistic countries, and their primary target has been the United States, the largest and most powerful capitalistic country, resulting in strong anti-business, anti-war, pro-abortion, and anti-capital punishment movements.

This perspective unfortunately bled a bit into the arguments incorporated in the formation of the current catechism, watering down the historic clarity the Catholic Church had presented to the world regarding capital punishment.

As the Church now beats back the minor degradation of Church doctrine influenced by liberation theology—a battle still joined—the clarity should return, particularly around the issues of protecting the life of the innocent through the just use of war and capital punishment.

There are many reasons for concern regarding this 'language sensitivity', chief being the relative lack of knowledge of criminal justice issues, given the thought that "bloodless means are sufficient to defend against the aggressor and to protect the safety of persons, public authority should limit itself to such means," which means, one assumes, refer to imprisonment in maximum security or super-max prisons, yet, we see several recent articles revealing how easily the imprisoned aggressor acts towards innocents outside of prison, beginning, as noted by Bykowicz (March 9, 2008):

> Now 28 years old, [....] has lived all but six months of his adult life behind bars. His home for the past four years, the Western Correctional Institution in Cumberland, is even farther from Baltimore — a place in which he might never have set foot. Yet authorities say they believe [he] commanded one of Baltimore's largest and most violent gangs....
>
> From his prison cell, according to a federal racketeering indictment last month, [he] enforced the gang's rules and oversaw its activities, including violent initiations, witness intimidation and five murders. (n.p.)

Another story from Ward (2008) notes how easily even death row prisoners are able to communicate, unfettered by supervision, with the outside world:

> [Texas] State prison officials, moving to address the headline-grabbing security breach caused by smuggled cell phones, on Wednesday proposed spending nearly $66 million on high-tech gear to curb contraband.

The plan is more than twice as costly as an earlier-announced plan to beef up security at Texas' 112 state prisons and is larger than several past programs to build prisons.

Smuggled cell phones have been an issue since October, when [a] death row convict ... was busted for possessing a phone on which more than 2,800 calls had been made in one month — including calls to a state senator. (n.p.)

Another article from North Carolina also addresses the cell phone issue. (Kane, 2008)

Cigarettes, drugs and booze used to drive a prison's black market economy. Today, state prison officials are trying to stop another item from being smuggled in — cell phones.

So far this year, the N.C. Department of Correction has confiscated roughly 140 cell phones that were found on inmates or stashed on prison grounds. The phones are considered contraband, but they are coming in anyway.

They arrive by visitors who sneak them in, by inmates returning from work release and, in some cases, by staff looking to make a fast buck. A $25 phone can sell for as much as $500 behind bars, prison officials say, and inmates who have them can charge others for their use.

Prisons director Boyd Bennett said the cell phones can be used for all kinds of mayhem in and out of prison. They can be used to set up attacks on inmates and staff, coordinate escapes, harass victims and allow criminals to continue running criminal enterprises outside prison. (n.p.)

And, yet another article about cell phones in California prisons, where Thompson (2009) notes:

Richard Subia, California's associate director for adult prisons, called cell phone use in state prisons "one of the most severe security issues that we have right now."

It's been a problem in prisons across the country.

A condemned inmate in Texas used a smuggled cell phone to make a threatening call to a state senator in October. Authorities say a drug dealer behind bars in Maryland used a phone to arrange to have a witness assassinated outside his home last summer.

In Kansas, a convicted killer sneaked out of prison after planning the 2006 escape using a cell phone smuggled by an accomplice. The following year, two inmates escaped another Kansas prison with the help of a former guard and a smuggled cell phone.

California prison officials confiscated about 2,800 cell phones statewide last year, double the number discovered the year before. Inmates can be punished for having them but have found ingenuous ways to hide them. (n.p.)

And yet one more from Fenton (2009):

The court records read like a scene out of *Goodfellas*: From their prison cells and with the help of corrections staff, authorities say, members of a violent gang were feasting on salmon and shrimp, sipping Grey Goose vodka and puffing fine cigars — all while directing drug deals, extorting protection money from other inmates and arranging attacks on witnesses and rival gang members...

A search warrant outlines how gang members were able to obtain heroin, direct hits on enemies through so-called "Death Angels" and conduct cell phone conference calls to arrange business with inmates around the state.

"It's not enough just to catch the bad guys and get them convicted and sent to prison," said Maryland U.S. Attorney Rod J. Rosenstein. "We need to make sure that while they're in prison, they're isolated and not able to carry on and continue their gang activities." (n.p.)

And finally from the Pelican Bay super-max in California, often considered the model of super-max facilities, Montgomery (n.d.) notes:

> Most of the inmates in the SHU are gang members. Their cells are windowless and nearly bare. The men are locked inside for 22 and a half hours a day, usually alone. They are held in virtual isolation to try to keep them from working together, but even the SHU can't stop some leaders from running their gangs...
>
> "The head leaders of [all the gangs] they're in prison," says [a Pelican Bay warden until 2004]. "And they control the activities of the gang both within the prison system and in our communities in California and now unfortunately, have even spread to other states." (n.p.)

Hopefully, the Catholic capital punishment abolition movement will reconsider their conclusion that other means—like life imprisonment or incarceration in super-max prisons—can protect the innocent from the aggressor, based on the porous nature of even the most secure of American prisons.

To further help explain the Church's change of the language around capital punishment over the past several decades, undoubtedly influenced by the atmosphere of the secular world, we can also turn to Fr. Charles (1998):

Secular liberalism, having rejected absolute moral truths and unchanging principles, inevitably degenerates into intellectual and moral anarchy or into a form of cultural totalitarianism. Where the political system is so weakened by events that in effect it collapses, as in inter-war Italy and Germany, the totalitarian state emerges. Where the society in which it is embedded is initially stronger, in time it falls into the former, as its strength is slowly sapped by skepticism and relativism, as it has been sapped in the Western democracies, and permissive selfishness takes over. The effects of this undermining of moral principles were staved off until the middle of this century by the continuing vitality of the old hierarchies of society, the paternalist family, the Church, the school, the law, the State. But the anarchy became more marked from the 1960's and has continued to gnaw away at the essential cultural code, any effective sense of right and wrong in the objective order, which any society needs to hand on to its children if they are to be formed into socially responsible citizens. (p. 194)

When we add to this the terrible disruption of the sexual scandal the Church began experiencing during that period, though not becoming public until much later, the unraveling of even the settled language, and the rearrangement of the dogmatic expression emanating from the Second Vatican Council, it is a wonder that as much of the hard truths that sustained the Church for the millennia, survived as strongly expressed as they have.

And this confusion was only compounded by the lack of leadership, resulting from the corruption of the sexual scandal, of those most responsible for providing teaching to the Church around the social teaching issues, noted by Lawler (2008):

> The same corruption that produced the sex-abuse scandal, the greatest crisis in the history of American Catholicism, remains widespread in the Church today. Indeed the corruption is more firmly entrenched now than it was in 2002 because the hierarchy has refused to acknowledge the most serious aspect of the scandal; the treason of the bishops. (p. 256)

Following up on that theme of the failure of the Church's leadership in their primary role of teaching, in a recent article, Lawler (February 2008) notes:

> Only a small minority of Catholic priests were engaged in sexual misconduct with young people, and now programs are in place to identify those predator-priests and remove them from active ministry. But a large *majority* of the American bishops were implicated in the effort to cover up clerical misconduct, and most of those delinquent bishops remain in office today, with their credibility in shreds.

Nothing could be more damaging to Church authority than the suspicion that bishops would mislead their own people. (n.p.)

Along with this degraded leadership, another weakness in the USCCB approach to capital punishment and other criminal justice issues, is a lack of professional knowledge from the field and an understanding of the Church's historic work around punishment and prisons, noted by Skotnicki (2002) referring to the 2000 statement on crime and criminal justice by the Catholic Bishops:

> The [USCCB] document [*Responsibility, Rehabilitation, and Restoration: A Catholic Perspective on Crime and Criminal Justice*] has notable flaws. It suffers not in its methodology but in the particular way that contemporary carceral experience and the foundational concepts of the Catholic social tradition are then invoked to support an incomplete and sometimes inaccurate analysis. (p. 147)

The support for abolishing capital punishment has long been part of the political left in the United States which the USCCB has moved in congruence with for a very long time, as Lawler (2008) notes:

> The newly emerging Church leaders [after Vatican II] seized every opportunity to lead their flock in a new direction. New social-action committees emerged at the parish

and diocesan levels. The U. S. Catholic Conference (later restructured to become the US Conference of Catholic Bishops) took on greater authority in Washington, lobbying politicians and generating nationwide support for various public initiatives. Almost without exception, the causes espoused by these Church groups were associated with the political left: disarmament, increased welfare spending, loose restrictions on immigration, and end to U.S. support for the authoritarian regimes that were battling Marxist guerillas in Latin America. (pp. 89-90)

Recently however, there are encouraging developments for a deeper understanding of criminal justice, social science, and Catholic historic contributions to it, in the work of the already mentioned Andrew Skotnicki, associate professor at Manhattan College, with his several related scholarly articles and two books: *Religion and the Development of the American Penal System* (2002) and *Criminal Justice and the Catholic Church* (2008); and the recent publication of the *Encyclopedia of Catholic Social Thought, Social Science and Social Policy* (2007) edited by Michael L. Coulter, Stephen M. Krason, Richard S. Myers, and Joseph A. Varacalli, and from the *Encyclopedia*, speaking of capital punishment, Rice, (2007), notes:

Pope John Paul II reaffirmed the traditional teaching that the state has the authority to impose the death penalty. His *Evangelium Vitae* and the *Catechism of the Catholic Church* have provided a new development of the teaching as to the *use* of that authority: The death penalty may rightly be imposed only *"if this is the only possible way of effectively defending human lives against the unjust aggressor.* If, however, non-lethal means are sufficient *to defend and protect people's safety from the aggressor, authority* will limit itself to such means, as these are more in keeping with the concrete conditions of the common good and more in conformity with the dignity of the human person.

...Under this teaching, a Catholic can rightly support the use of the death penalty only in cases that satisfy the enhanced requirement of absolute necessity, when it would not be possible otherwise to defend society. This criterion refers not to some generalized protection of society by promoting respect for law or by deterring potential offenders through fear of the death penalty, but rather to protection of society "from the aggressor," that is, *from this convicted criminal.*
(Vol. 1, pp. 282-283)

It is from the examination of protecting society "from this convicted criminal", that the Lampstand Foundation considers the proper use of the death penalty as a legitimate sanction for serial pedophiles and serial rapists.

Policy

Perhaps what is most marked about the position of the social teaching in the United States—and many others who study it—is the generally accepted assumption that the Church's work in this area began with the 1891 encyclical of Pope Leo XIII.

The difficulty with relying on this perception is that much of the foundational work of the social teaching—coming from the Old Testament and medieval sources—is not factored in, resulting in a skewed result.

This is particularly true with capital punishment, prisons, and punishment in general, which saw much of its most articulate principles developed during those periods, well documented by the work of Rodger Charles and Andrew Skotnicki.

The publication of the USCCB *Catechism* (2006), noted the position that capital punishment "cannot be justified".

> When dwelling on legal and moral arguments concerning the death penalty, we should do so not with vengeance and anger in our hearts, but with the compassion and mercy of our Lord in mind. It is also important to remember that penalties imposed on criminals always need to allow for the possibility of the criminal to show

regret for the evil committed and to change his or her life for the better.

The imposition of the death penalty does not always allow for one or both of the purposes of criminal punishment to be achieved. "Our nation's increasing reliance on the death penalty cannot be justified. We do not teach that killing is wrong by killing those who kill others. Pope John Paul II has said the penalty of death is 'both cruel and unnecessary' (Homily in St. Louis January 27, 1999). The antidote to violence is not more violence." USSB, *Faithful Citizenship* 2003, 19) (pp. 394-395)

The reasons given by the USCCB (2005) for why we should abolish capital punishment are:

Our nation should forgo the use of the death penalty because

- The sanction of death, when it is not necessary to protect a society, violates respect for human life and dignity.
- State-sanctioned killing in our names diminishes all of us.
- Its application is deeply flawed and can be irreversibly wrong, is prone to errors, and is biased by factors such as race, the quality of legal representation, and where the crime was committed.

- We have other ways to punish criminals and protect society. (p. 3)

What is not included here is the central aspect of Catholic anthropology concerning criminal acts, the agency of free individuals to commit evil acts, and as we shall see in the next section regarding the approach of Pope Pius XII, the traditional teaching of the Church about capital punishment is based upon that anthropology.

Flannery (2007) quoting Dewan, notes how *being* criminal impacts the morality of murder and capital punishment:

> Specifically, speaking of the way the "circumstance" of a person's being a criminal alters the moral character of the act of killing, Dewan says:
>
> > That the man executed is a criminal adds [to the act of execution] a circumstance of the sort which constitutes a new and good rational order. To shy from this is simply to doubt reason's ability to recognize good order for human life. Thus, people who fail to recognize the difference of the two species [murder and execution] might be suffering from a blindness as regards the primacy of the common good. (n. 45 Flannery p. 409)

Budziszewski (2004) addresses the retributive reasoning of the organized abolition movement in the United States.

> Now, the argument against capital punishment works like this. True, the purpose of retribution is served by the murderer's death, but under certain circumstances retribution might interfere with other purposes of punishment. It might prematurely put an end to his rehabilitation, it might undermine deterrence by inciting wicked men to greater evils, and it might not be necessary for the safety of others. Therefore, it would be better not to kill him, but to protect society by other means—perhaps to lock him up forever. The difficulty with this argument is that it seems to regard the secondary purposes of punishment as sufficient to overturn its primary purpose. If rehabilitation, protection, and deterrence cannot justify doing more than what retribution demands, how can they justify doing less? (p. 111)

Determining the evolution of abolitionist thinking by the USCCB from advocates of the Church's traditional support of capital punishment to advocates for its abolition, is beyond the scope of this book, but we might discern some vestiges of roots in the movement around the issue of abortion, the other major issue involving the protection of the innocent that has seen a substantial shift in political perception and action—

at least by the Democratic party—in the United States.

This shift is examined by Hendershott (2006) and she notes a transformative meeting:

> In a long-forgotten meeting at the Kennedy compound in Hyannisport, on a hot summer day in 1964, the Kennedy family and their advisers and allies were coached by leading theologians and Catholic college professors to accept and promote abortion with a "clear conscience." Albert Jonsen, a former Jesuit, recalls how this happened.
>
> > In July, 1964, Jesuit priest, Fr. Joseph Fuchs, renowned Catholic moral theologian and a professor at the Gregorian University in Rome,... and I, the American novice, traveled to Cape Cod to join Catholic theologians, Fr. Robert Drinan, the dean of Boston College Law School; Fr. Richard McCormick, Fr. Charles Curran...
>
> Another Jesuit who helped redefine abortion for the Kennedy family at that meeting in Hyannisport was Fr. Giles Milhaven, who later recalled at a 1984 breakfast meeting of Catholics for a Free Choice:
>
> > The theologians worked for a day and a half among ourselves at a nearby

hotel. In the evening we answered questions from the Kennedys and the Shrivers. Though the theologians disagreed on many a point, they concurred on certain basics...and that was that a Catholic politician could in good conscience vote in favor of abortion. (pp. 10-11)

The results of this meeting are clear and we have seen many Catholic politicians attempt to make the same case.

The USCCB Statement (2005) was clear that they were not formulating new doctrine, noting:

In these pastoral reflections, we do not offer new teaching or doctrine but rather hope to help Catholics better understand and apply this teaching in our own time and situation. (p. 4)

However, many of the faithful do now believe that it is the doctrine of the Church that capital punishment should be abolished, though fortunately, the majority feels otherwise.

The cloudy thinking around the current position, the obvious lack of input from Catholic supporters of capital punishment, and the change in language from the 1992 Catechism to the 1997 Catechism, is a reminder that, as deeply as we should respect our bishops and continually pray for them, there are times when we should respond to the canonical teaching from the Canon Law Society of America (1983):

> 212-3. According to the knowledge, competence, and prestige which they possess, they have the right and even at times the duty to manifest to the sacred pastors their opinion on matters which pertain to the good or the Church and to make their opinion known to the rest of the Christian faithful, without prejudice to the integrity of faith and morals, with reverence toward their pastors, and attentive to common advantage and the dignity of persons. (Section 212-3)

Pope Pius XII

Pope Pius XII (1876-1958) was the last modern pope to have spoken extensively on capital punishment—in two major speeches to jurists and doctors—and throughout his papacy he continued to comment on crime and punishment, and it is here we can look for modern papal validation of the ancient tradition of the Catholic Church's support for capital punishment.

Pius was a singularly talented pope and his effectiveness was reflected in the skill with which he kept the Nazi's at bay when they occupied Rome, saving thousands of Jews he had hidden away in the Vatican and other Church buildings, and in the post war attempt by the Communist government of the Soviet Union to destroy him, an attempt that was partially successful, and it is only now, almost 50 years after his death, that the full story is coming out as he approaches canonization.

Pius became Pope in 1939, six months before the outbreak of World War II. He was very learned and came from a family—and developed a personal background—in the law, as noted by Krause (2007);

> His father was a lawyer in the Congregation of the Sacred Rota...In 1893 he [Pius] entered the Caprancia College to begin his seminary training, and took courses at the Gregorian University. He was ordained a priest in 1899. He earned doctorates in philosophy and theology, and became fluent in German, French, and English.
>
> Entering the papal secretariat of state in 1901, he became a close collaborator of Cardinal Gasparri in the task of revising and updating the *Code of Canon Law*. (p. 853)

Hunt (2007) notes the central role Pius played in formulating the modern response to crime:

> The Catholic Church holds a much broader understanding of the mystery of evil and natural law [than criminologists]. While this understanding rests on centuries of Catholic scholarship, the contours of this understanding can be found in Pope Pius XII's 1954 address on "Crime and

Punishment" to the Italian Association of Catholic Jurists. (Vol. 1, p.257)

Pius said in that 1954 address:

> The criminal act is furthermore always an opposition of one person to another, both when the immediate object of the act is an actual person, as in murder, and when this object is a thing, as in theft; ... setting itself up in opposition to a higher Authority and therefore ultimately against the Authority of God. (Pope Pius XII (1961) p. 307)

Pius XII, in keeping with the ancient tradition of the Church, reaffirmed that legitimate defense often required the taking of life and in a talk to physicians in September 1952, Pope Pius XII (1961) said:

> Even when there is question of the execution of a condemned man, the state does not dispose of the individual's right to life. In this case, it is reserved to the public power to deprive the condemned person of the enjoyment of life in expiation of his crime when, by his crime, he has already disposed himself of his right to live. (pp. 232-233)

Pope Pius XII (1957) spoke of respect for the law and that it is ultimately, based on faith in God:

> Who would have thought that following the proud peak of civilization and culture which

has been the boast of preceding generations, respect for law would encounter perils, trials, and violations such as only the darkest periods of history have known? But even in such matters the key to every solution is given by faith in a personal God, Who is fount of justice and has reserved to Himself the right over life and death. Nothing else but this faith can confer the moral force to observe the proper limits in the face of all insidious temptations to overstep them; keeping in mind that, excepting in cases of legitimate defense, of just war fought with just means and of capital punishment inflicted by the public authority for well-determined and proven gravest crimes, human life is intangible. (pp. 227-228)

What is marked through Pope Pius XII's teaching is its congruence with the Catholic anthropology of individual responsibility, while the reason given for the abolitionist's position, is not.

While we are certainly bound by the magisterium of Pope John Paul II that capital punishment may only be used after the conditions expressed in the Catechism have been met, that is largely the existing situation already, and rather than calling for an abolition as the USCCB have, the retention of the traditional response of the Church, which Pope John Paul II also reaffirms, is rightly mandated within the Catechism.

The value of the magisterium of Pope Pius XII has

been deepening as time allows further study of it, and that was remarked on by Pope Benedict XVI (2008) when he said:

> I have admired the demanding theme on which you have concentrated your attention. In the last years, when one spoke of Pius XII, the attention was drawn in an excessive way to only one issue, considered, moreover, in a rather unilateral manner. Every other consideration aside, this has impeded an adequate approach to the figure of great historical-theological depth that Pope Pius XII has been. The convergence of the impressive activity that took place during this Pontificate and, in a singular way, his Magisterium on what you have considered in these days is an eloquent proof of what I just affirmed. Indeed, his Magisterium is characterized for the vast and beneficent breadth, and also for his exceptional quality, such that one cannot fail to say that it constitutes a precious heritage of which the Church has and continues to treasure. (para. 2)

A handicap present among some within the Church leadership is that they may not have encountered unrepentant human evil, but Pope Pius XII was not so handicapped, as he dealt for decades with one of the most evil assemblages of human beings in history—the Nazi regime—and had seen through the often charming exteriority of those evil men, witnessing their true interiority, and this vision gives his reflections on the ancient support of the teaching of capital punishment enhanced credibility.

Conclusion

𝔉or much of human history, the social value of human beings in the pagan world was barely above that of other objects, and this extreme devaluing of persons undergirded the pagan practice of capital punishment.

This is revealed around the response by citizens of the Roman Empire to two issues, abortion and slavery, noted by Aries and Duby (1987):

> The birth of a Roman was not merely a biological fact. Infants came into the world, or at any rate were received into society, only as the head of the family willed. Contraception, abortion, the exposure of freeborn infants, and infanticide of slaves' children were common and perfectly legal practices...Immediately after the birth it was the father's prerogative to raise the child from the earth where the midwife had placed it, thus indicating that he recognized the infant as his own and declined to expose it...A child whose father did not raise it up was exposed outside the house or in some public place. (p. 9)
>
> ....The slave was inferior by nature, whatever he was or did. This natural inferiority went

hand in hand with legal inferiority. ...If the master, who had the right to punish a slave at will, decided that he deserved the ultimate punishment, he would hire the municipal executioner to do the job, paying only the cost of the pitch and sulfur needed to burn the unfortunate victim. (p. 59)

Slavery continued, though denounced by word and practice within the moral development of the Judeo-Christian world, and the value of individual human beings increased—especially those of the innocent—as they were children of God, created in his divine image.

The history of the protection of the common good, by the state, through the use of judicially applied capital punishment is noted by Hardon (1999) in his *Modern Catholic Dictionary*:

> It is certain from scripture that civil authorities may lawfully put malefactors to death. Capital punishment was enacted for certain grievous crimes in the Old law, e.g., blasphemy, sorcery, adultery, and murder. Christian dispensation made no essential changes in this respect, as St. Paul expressly says: "The state is there to serve God for your benefit. If you break the law, however, you may well have fear; the bearing of the sword has its significance" (Romans 13:4). Among the errors of the Waldenses condemned by the Church in the early

thirteenth century was the proposition that denied the lawfulness of capital punishment.

St. Thomas Aquinas (1225-74) defends capital punishment on the grounds of the common good. The state, he reasons, is like a body composed of many members, and as a surgeon may cut off one corrupt limb to save the others, so the civil authority may lawfully put a criminal to death and thus provide for the common good....

In principle, however, it is morally licit because in the most serious crimes the claims of retribution and deterrence are so demanding that the corrective value of punishment must, if necessary, be sacrificed. (p. 81)

In our reflections on the social teaching we want to use our historical perspective with a realization of the evolving nature of the teaching in relation to that of social development, well expressed by William Buckley in this interview with Michael Cromartie (1997):

[Cromartie] Once when defining conservatism you said it is the "tacit acknowledgement that all that is finally important in human experience is behind us." What did you mean?

[Buckley] I wrote that in 1957. What I meant was that it is inconceivable to me as a

Christian that God forgot to say critical things, or if there was anything terrifically important, it's hard to think that Jesus would have forgotten to pass it along. Obviously, there are lots of refinements on the Ten Commandments and the creed. But in terms of importance what has been said is what is important. All the rest is exegesis and development. (n.p.)

We see this played out in the teaching around capital punishment, as the Old Testament and the teachings of the medieval Fathers describe many occasions when it may be applied, yet it has developed such that today it is called for rarely.

The new language of the Church has the right pitch, expressing compassion for the executed, as is proper, while clearly retaining the authority to execute, and this is congruent with the Church's thinking defined by Hardon (1999):

> **Development of Doctrine**. Growth in the Church's understanding of the truths of divine revelation. Also called dogmatic process or dogmatic development, it is the gradual unfolding of the meaning of what God has revealed. Always presumed is that the substantial truth of a revealed mystery remains unchanged. What changes is the subjective grasp of the revealed truth.
>
> The source of this progressive understanding is the prayerful reflection of

the faithful, notably of the Church's saints and mystics; the study and research by scholars and theologians; the practical experience of living the faith among the faithful; and the collective wisdom and teaching of the Church's hierarchy under the Bishop of Rome.

Implicit in the development of doctrine is the will of God that the faithful not only assent to what he revealed but also grow in the depth, clarity, and certitude of their appropriation of divine faith. (p. 155)

God was very clear in what he revealed, both at Sinai and soon after his transfiguration, when he taught his disciples about scandal, that the death of the evildoer is often justified when the physical or spiritual life of the innocent is involved.

The historical tradition of the Church has always and continues to support the use of capital punishment, and yet, we should always use it carefully, compassionately, justly, and treating even the evildoer with the dignity and respect his humanity has received from God.

Obviously, not all Catholic leaders support capital punishment, and many of them who are calling for abolition do so based partly on arguments of cruelty, but it is not cruelty to execute the aggressor when that is the only option to protect the innocent; rather it is the power to say, *Stop, you shall no longer harm the innocent,* for if we are not willing to support the use of the power of the state to stop the aggressor from harming the innocent, we become complicit in that harm.

Regarding the prevalent objections to capital punishment forming the core of the abolitionists argument, Budziszewski (2004) concluded:

> Our brief review of the objections to capital punishment has left the interim conclusion unshaken.
>
> 1. In considering whether to grant clemency, the proper question is not whether juries ever err, but whether we have reasonable ground to think that *this* jury has erred in fact.
> 2. Any deserved punishment, indeed any element of justice, might whet the impulse for revenge. But when a good impulse is perverted, we should fight not the impulse but its perversion; and so with the impulse for justice.
> 3. Scripture and Christian tradition uphold capital punishment not in contempt for life but in reverence for it. It is *because* man is made in God's image that Torah decrees that whoever sheds the blood of man, by man shall his blood be shed.
> 4. Christ did teach personal forgiveness, but he never challenged the need for public justice. Official pardon rightly has conditions which personal forgiveness does not. Not only is punishment

compatible with love, it is sometimes demanded by it as the only medicine strong enough to do the offender good. (pp. 121-122)

It is noteworthy that some of the Catholic leaders who worked on softening the opposition to abortion, also worked on softening the support of capital punishment, and one participant in the formulation of abortion political policy, Fr. Drinan, had called for the abolition of capital punishment in the United States since the 1950's.

This is the same Fr. Drinan who offered theological support to the speaker of the United States House of Representatives, Nancy Pelosi, in her many pro-abortion actions, noted by Ertelt (2009):

Pelosi describes herself as an "ardent" Catholic but the San Francisco-based congresswoman has taken a consistent pro-abortion stance in defiance of Catholic pro-life teachings.

She has a long-time pro-abortion voting record, according to the National Right to Life Committee, and has repeatedly voted against a ban on partial-birth abortions and against efforts to stop direct taxpayer funding of abortions....

Deal Hudson, a respected Catholic author and journalist, commented on the Pelosi visit....

Hudson says Pelosi has a long relationship with dissident Catholics and pointed to her relationship with Rev. Robert Drinan, who she chose as the celebrant of the Mass held in her honor when she became Speaker in January 2006.

"The late Father Drinan, a longtime professor of law at Georgetown University, had been the architect of the arguments now used as cover by Catholic politicians who wish to dodge the abortion issue," Hudson said. "This effort began in 1964, when Father Drinan was among a small group of theologians who visited Hyannis Port, Massachusetts, to school the Kennedy clan on how to finesse the abortion issue in politics." (n.p.)

The involvement of Catholics in politics is commented on by the perceptive French nobleman, and devout Catholic, Alexis de Tocqueville (1805-1859) who wrote one of the truly great books, *Democracy in America,* that readers continue to mine for intelligent analysis of our American way of life, and here is what he had to say about Catholic priests involved in politics in America in the 19th century:

It often happened that the Catholic priest left the sanctuary to enter society as a power, and that he came to seat himself there amid the social hierarchy; then sometimes he used his religious influence to assure the longevity of a political order of which he was a part; then also one could see Catholics become partisans of aristocracy by the spirit of religion....

The Catholic clergy of the United States has not tried to struggle against this political tendency; rather, it seeks to justify it. Catholic priests in America have divided the intellectual world into two parts: in one, they have left revealed dogmas, and they submit to them without discussing them; in the other, they have placed political truth, and they think that God has abandoned it to the free inquiries of men. Thus Catholics in the United States are at once the most submissive of the faithful and the most independent of citizens. (pp. 276-277)

I do not feel the problems around the confusion on the formally clear teaching of the Church about capital punishment to necessarily be the fault of any particular priest or bishop, or their particular allegiance to any political party; but rather the general bending to the influence of the most ancient heresy all of us who are human struggle against; that we sometimes feel we don't need God, and we can make the decisions about primary things on our own, which always leads to sin, which always creates confusion, and which only the grace of a forgiving God, and the reaching out of a penitent soul can undo.

I believe that the gist of the current confusion arose from a reductionist view of some sections of the encyclical *Evangelium Vitae*, by Pope John Paul II, where, while it appeared to be a development of the doctrine around capital punishment, it in fact was not.

Long (1999) notes:

> The encyclical's generally negative evaluation of recourse to the death penalty (which is undoubted), when construed doctrinally, is often thought to present so apparent a disparity with the traditional doctrine as to suggest that a new element has been introduced in the consideration of the death penalty that would trump all the traditional arguments. Specifically, it might be thought that a development of doctrine regarding the *transcendent value of life* could supply a premise for dissociating life from the general principles governing retributive justice. If such an argument were made in *Evangelium vitae,* it would then be possible to assess this argument vis-à-vis the tradition. If the argument proved sufficient, then there would indeed be a ground to reject the general norms of retributive punishment in the unique case of the death penalty while retaining them for lesser penalties. Even so, the coherence of this position would be difficult to sustain, as analogical proportionality would then not be sustained betwixt life and the lesser but

profound goods of freedom, social integration, and so on—for the penalties touching each of these is contrary to a distinct good of nature, and so seemingly should be proportionally subject to the same principles (howsoever profound the differences). Yet in any case such an argument is not made; nor is it clear that any argument superordinating physical survival to justice can be consistent with either Scripture or tradition (clearly the most sublime sacrifice of life ever made—on the cross—is made in mercy to satisfy justice). Nor, lastly, are we now in possession of any principle that exempts human life as such from the general norms of retributive penalty. (pp. 537-538)

Part of the work of the Lampstand Foundation was the creation of criminal justice principles, (see Appendix), and our fourth principle is: "Capital punishment is an appropriate response to the criminal evil of murder, rape, and pedophilia."

Capital punishment for sexual abuse is not something unknown in the history of the Church, indeed Matthew 18:6 obviously concerns it as an especially evil aspect of scandal, but more specifically, St. Pope Pius V felt it to be an appropriate deterrent, as noted by Lawler, (2008):

In 1568 Pope Pius V lamented that the papal states had been "polluted" by sexual abuse. To curtail this "detestable monstrosity," he ruled that any priest found guilty of sexual abuse should be stripped of his clerical status and privilege and handed over to the secular courts. The secular courts were likely to punish their offenses by the death penalty: a prospect that did not worry the Pontiff at all. On the contrary Pius V—today known as *Saint* Pius V—said that severe punishment would send a useful message to other clerics who might be tempted to prey on children. He calmly observed that "whoever does not abhor the ruination of the soul, the avenging secular sword of civil law will certainly deter." (pp. 137-138)

Recently, the 1950's era letters of Rev. Gerald Fitzgerald, founder of the Servants of the Paraclete—who treated priests guilt of sexual abuse—reveals just how evil he felt this activity was, as noted by Dunklin (2009):

One of Fitzgerald's strategies for dealing with the priests, upon whom "the wrath of God is," was isolating them on an island in Barbados.

He had made a down payment on the property but was later forced to sell it when a new bishop wanted out of the ownership.

"It is for this class of rattlesnake I have always wished for the island retreat," Fitzgerald wrote to an unidentified bishop in 1957."But even an island is too good for these vipers of whom the Gentle Master said—it were better they had not been born." (n.p.)

The Church founded by Christ has stood alone against the world for millennia, speaking truth to power, always the same truth with different voices, and though, as a humanly managed institution on earth has often stumbled—even as Peter stumbled—the clarity of its truth remains triumphant.

Capital punishment, blood for blood, just retribution upon the aggressor who slays the innocent physically or spiritually, has been a central part of that truth and though confusion about the traditional support for it has arisen over the past few decades, the repository of faith expressed in the Catechism still includes that support—though in the 1997 second edition of the Catechism has been expressed as a negative, rather than the positive of the first edition of 1992.

While the "oldest Roman catechism" (Holy See 1997, #196) is the apostles creed; the universal catechisms are the primary sources, and there have been two—which are truly only one—that of Pope Pius V, published in 1566 from the work of the Council of Trent (1545-1563), and that of Pope John Paul II, published in 1997 (2nd Ed.) from the work of the Second Vatican Council (1962-1965).

Discovering and living the truth of God's word in the cloud of the word of the world is part of the cross we bear, and though Christ called us to his path of being a sign of contradiction to the world, we are afraid, and we wish to live in peace with the world, so we choose peace in one battle while fighting others—an often wise strategy even sanctioned by the holy spirit and the apostles—for did not St. Paul instruct us in the craft of conversion.

Yet in learning and adopting the same lessons to become proficient in the craft of conversion, we also need to remain adept in the knowledge of truth and it is to know the nature of those for whom capital punishment has been proclaimed—for they are not of the faithful but outside, outlaws—as a response to criminal evil from the beginning of the Church, that we can learn from the first universal catechism, the Roman Catechism (1566), which states:

> Of these remedies the most efficacious is to form a just conception of the wickedness of murder. The enormity of this sin is manifest from many and weighty passages of Holy Scripture. So much does God abominate homicide that He declares in Holy Writ that of the very beast of the field He will exact vengeance for the life of man, commanding the beast that injures man to be put to death. And if (the Almighty) commanded man to have a horror of blood,' He did so for no other reason than to impress on his mind the obligation of entirely refraining, both in

act and desire, from the enormity of homicide.

The murderer is the worst enemy of his species, and consequently of nature. To the utmost of his power he destroys the universal work of God by the destruction of man, since God declares that He created all things for man's sake. Nay, as it is forbidden in Genesis to take human life, because God created man to his own image and likeness, he who makes away with God's image offers great injury to God, and almost seems to lay violent hands on God Himself! (pp. 224-225)

As we come to the end of our journey through the 5th commandment, the great *not* in the Great Commandment of neighborly love, we know that for sound guidance and the final word, we must—in addition to maintaining our daily practice of prayer and communion—look to the Magisterium, we must look to the Holy Father, we must look to the Holy See, we must look to the Universal Catechism, we must look to the center, for truly, the center holds.

Afterword

Speculating on how it has come to be that this seemingly most clear of the ancient sanctions of the Church, that is—along with just war—a central part of the protection of the innocent from the aggressor, has come to be so hotly contested in the last days of the second millennium, leads us into deep waters, and though we are in danger of drowning in the cesspool of the results of the attacks on the Church from within and without, we must not avert our gaze, for it is often in confrontation of the dark face of evil that the force of truth shines most brightly.

I mentioned the Albigensian Heresy in the foreword and how they, along with other heretics, stood against war and capital punishment.

Belloc (1991) describes the roots of the Albigensian Heresy:

> The Albigensian attack was but the chief of a great number, all of which drew their source from the Manichean conception of a duality in the Universe; the conception that good and evil are ever struggling as equals, and that Omnipotent Power is neither single nor beneficent. Closely intertwined with this idea and inseparable from it was the conception that matter is evil and that all pleasure, especially of the body, is evil. This form of attack, of which I say the Albigensian was the most notorious and

came nearest to success, was rather an attack upon morals than upon doctrine; it had the character of a cancer fastening upon the body of the Church from within, producing a new life of it own, antagonistic to the life of the Church and destructive of it—just as a malignant growth in the human body lives a life of its own, other than, and destructive of, the organism in which it has parasitically arisen. (pp. 11-12)

This rejection of everything the Catholic Church stands for corresponds to the conclusion reached by Belloc (1991) about the nature of the great heresies stemming from Manicheism, when describing Albigensianism as it played out in 12th Century France:

How much that culture was imperiled [by the Albigensians] can be seen from the main tenets which were openly preached and acted upon. All the sacraments were abandoned. In their place a strange ritual was adopted, mixed up with fire worship, called "The Consolation," in which it was professed that the soul was purified. The propagation of mankind was attacked; marriage was condemned, and the leaders of the sect spread all the extravagances which you find hovering around Manicheism or Puritanism wherever it appears. Wine was evil, meat was evil, war was always absolutely wrong, so was capital punishment; but the one unforgivable sin was reconciliation with the Catholic Church. There again the Albigensians were true to type. All heresies make that their chief point. (pp. 90-91)

And here is where we might discover the truth about the resistance to capital punishment coupled with a political acceptance of abortion that grew so fervently in America, that in the mid-twentieth century, some among the Catholic leadership in America that appeared to be traditionally orthodox in their words, were actually completely opposite in their actions, as they acted as vicious predators upon the flock they vowed to protect and shepherd.

As such they were in a long line of evil or frightened men acting within the sanctuary of the Church to destroy her, even in the very beginning with those around Christ, for did not one betray him, one deny him, and nine ran from him, so that at the crucifixion only the three Marys and the apostle John remained.

And though we must take the opposition to capital punishment at face value, we can also understand the context from which it emanates and speculate as to its origin, and it surely appears to be from dissent; a dissent that appears to be attempting to stimulate a perverse development of the ancient doctrine, not only of the right of secular authorities to utilize capital punishment to protect the innocent, but also the just use of war; and if this development of doctrine succeeds it will be another tearing of the holy fabric of precious material from earth and heaven of the great cathedral of our Holy Mother Church.

Within the Church is a battleground, the ancient battleground of evil fighting its eternally losing battle against our Risen Lord, and what the reading and studying of the horrors of predatory religious upon the youth of our Church, has led me to, is a deeper knowledge of the truth of the faith, and a deeper connection to the importance of maintaining a strong and consistent devotional and prayer life *for* the Church; for she will surely prevail, though the gates of hell are arrayed against her, within and without, she will prevail.

Yes, our great Church will prevail, and she will also take her time in mulling over teaching emanating from Councils that appear to be reshaped to be more congruent with the signs of the times, and it may be the case with capital punishment.

Dulles (2007) commenting on reception as interpretation, wrote:

> It often takes several generations before a consensus is reached or before the Magisterium itself issues an authentic interpretation. For example, there was considerable doubt for some years about the precise import of the term *homoousion* ("consubstantial") as used by Nicaea. Many interpreted it in a semi-Arian sense until the Council of Constantinople in 381 upheld the

strict interpretation given by Athanasius and his party.

> The interpretation of Vatican II has been a source of great concern over the past generation. Some interpretations placed that council in sharp opposition to Trent, Vatican I, and popes such as Pius XII. Foreseeing the likelihood that collegiality would be misunderstood in a parliamentarian sense, Paul VI wisely insisted on appending the "Prefatory Note of Explanation" to the third chapter of *Lumen gentium.* (p. 108)

It has only been a little over ten years since the change was made in the words describing capital punishment between the First and Second Edition of the *Catechism,* and while much thought and discussion has already arisen, it will certainly continue to be so for this ancient sanction of the People of God to protect the innocent; and it may be, as Pope John Paul II (1993) taught us:

> The Council also encouraged theologians, "while respecting the methods and requirements of theological science, to look for *a more appropriate way of communicating* doctrine to the people of their time; since there is a difference between the deposit or the truths of faith and the manner in which they are expressed, keeping the same meaning and the same judgment". (#29)

APPENDIX

The Lampstand Foundation Guiding Criminal Justice Principles

Capital punishment is an appropriate response to the criminal evil of murder, rape, and pedophilia.

Introduction

Ⓞur organization's concern is the criminal justice system in the United States and these criminal justice principles will help guide our work in that regard.

The formal foundation of Judeo-Christian criminal justice principles was established in Exodus 20:22 to 23:20, the *Book of the Covenant*.

It is described by Navarre (1999):

> This collection of laws is usually described as the "Book of the Covenant" on account of what is said in 24:7, or the "Code of the Covenant", because many of these laws are similar to those to be found in legal codes of Semitic peoples, such as the Sumerian code of Ur-Nammu (c. 2050 BC), that of Esnunna

(c. 1950 BC), that of Lipit-Istar (c. 1850 BC) and (the most famous) code of Hammurabi (c. 1700 BC), which is conserved on a dioritic stone in the Louvre Museum, Paris.

The laws collected here probably existed earlier in a similar or even identical wording, but by being inserted into the Book of the Covenant in the context of the events of Sinai they acquire extra weight and authority. They become as it were the "basic laws" of the people, ratified by God himself. (Navarre University (1999): *The Navarre Bible: The Pentateuch, commentary by members of the faculty of theology of the University of Navarre.* Princeton, NJ: Scepter Publishers. p. 331)

1) Broken windows policing works.

Allowing even the minor violation of a broken window in an area helps create the impression of an environment where law and order does not prevail and where crime flourishes. Responding quickly and efficiently to all crimes, regardless of the perceived state of seriousness or other local community concerns, is the foundation of good police work.

The Vatican Catechism (2007) teaches:

> **2266** The State's effort to contain the spread of behaviors injurious to human rights and the fundamental rules of civil

coexistence corresponds to the requirement of watching over the common good.

2) The response to crime should be swift, balanced, and just.

When justice is for sale, either through wealth, influence, or ideology, a fertile soil is created from which crime grows. The training and education of professionals in the criminal justice system is built on a foundation of traditional and well-reasoned concepts of justice and it needs continual reinforcement to remain an effective response to crime.

> You shall do no injustice in judgment; you shall not be partial to the poor or defer to the great, but in righteousness shall you judge your neighbor. (Leviticus 19:15)

3) Prison is the most appropriate criminal sanction to protect society and punish the criminal, while allowing the opportunity for criminal reformation.

Prison is an effective sanction for crime which has been used by human beings since ancient times. It serves to protect the public from predatory crime, acts as a deterrence and as incapacitation, and allows the penitential criminal the opportunity—while removed from the community—to reflect upon and correct his criminal behavior.

From the U. S. Bishops (2006):

> **468.** A punishment imposed by legitimate public authority has the aim of redressing the disorder introduced by the offense, of defending public order and people's safety, and contributing to the correction of the guilty party. (*Compendium: Catechism of the Catholic Church.* Washington, *D.C.* United States Conference of Catholic Bishops. p. 137)

4) Capital punishment is an appropriate response to the criminal evil of murder, rape, and pedophilia.

Capital punishment is often the only effective social method available to protect the innocent and applied with dispatch after legal review of the crimes charged and determining the fitness of its application, should be considered an appropriate sentence for murderers, rapists and pedophiles; who, knowing the time of their death, are able, with certainty of their remaining time to do so, seek God's forgiveness.

Five states, as of May 2008, already approve the use of capital punishment in child rape cases: Louisiana, Montana, Oklahoma, South Carolina, and Texas.

From the Vatican Catechism (2007):

2267 The traditional teaching of the Church does not exclude, presupposing full ascertainment of the identity and responsibility of the offender, recourse to the death penalty, when this is the only practicable way to defend the lives of human beings effectively against the aggressor.

From the Summa Theologia (1920)

Reply to Objection 2. As the Philosopher observes (Ethic. ix, 3), when our friends fall into sin, we ought not to deny them the amenities of friendship, so long as there is hope of their mending their ways, and we ought to help them more readily to regain virtue than to recover money, had they lost it, for as much as virtue is more akin than money to friendship. When, however, they fall into very great wickedness, and become incurable, we ought no longer to show them friendliness. It is for this reason that both Divine and human laws command such like sinners to be put to death, because there is greater likelihood of their harming others than of their mending their ways. Nevertheless the judge puts this into effect, not out of hatred for the sinners, but out of the love of charity, by reason of which he prefers the public good to the life of the individual. Moreover the death inflicted by the judge profits the sinner, if he be converted, unto the expiation of his crime; and, if he be not converted, it profits so as to put an end to the sin, because the sinner is thus deprived of the power to sin any more. (St. Thomas Aquinas, Summa Theologica II II, Ques. 25, Article 6, reply to objection 2. Retrieved March 15, 2008 from http://www.newadvent.org/summa/3025.ht m)

Reply to Objection 2. According to the order of His wisdom, God sometimes slays sinners forthwith in order to deliver the good, whereas sometimes He allows them time to repent, according as He knows what is expedient for His elect. This also does human justice imitate according to its powers; for it puts to death those who are dangerous to others, while it allows time for repentance to those who sin without grievously harming others. (St. Thomas Aquinas, Summa Theologica II-II Ques. 64 Article 2, reply to objection 2. Retrieved March 15, 2008 from http://www.newadvent.org/summa/3064.h tm#article2)

5) Repentant criminals deserve a second chance.

$\mathfrak{E}$xcepting those cases of serious predatory behavior deserving the death penalty or natural life in prison, repentant criminals, once they have clearly shown—over a ten year period after being released from criminal justice supervision—that they have transformed their life by becoming a productive member of their family, their church, their vocation, and their community, should be allowed to apply for a complete pardon in a simple straightforward process.

From Caesar forgiveness may be sought but is rarely given, but from God forgiveness is always given. The Vatican Catechism (2007) teaches:

> **982** There is no offense, however serious, that the Church cannot forgive. There is no one, however wicked and guilty, who may not confidently hope for forgiveness, provided his repentance is honest. Christ who died for all men desires that in his Church the gates of forgiveness should always be open to anyone who turns away from sin.

6) It takes a reformed criminal to reform criminals.

$\mathfrak{F}$or generations the ability of non-criminals—even those with the highest professional and academic credentials—to effectively rehabilitate criminals has proven, based on sound evaluations, to be virtually non-existent. Recruiting reformed criminals who have, through education, training, and the development of a deep knowledge leadership approach to criminal transformation, may well succeed where others have failed. Considering the current recidivism rate of 70%, and with the consensus that peer-based help does, at the very least, attract those who want help to transformative programs, it is time to try this approach in a substantial enough way, over time and properly evaluated, to discover if we can rely on it as a valuable tool for large-scale implementation.

As I've written:

> Transformed criminals with advanced degrees and Catholic social teaching knowledge—I describe as deep knowledge leaders—working through grassroots community organizations, can help reverse the long-term failure of criminal rehabilitation programs, as they possess the elemental experiential knowledge of the criminal world allowing them, and them only, the authentic access to criminals long denied the social work professional. (Lukenbill, D. H. (2006). *The criminal's search for God: Criminal transformation, Catholic social teaching, deep knowledge leadership, and communal reentry.* Sacramento, CA: Chulu Press, LampStand Foundation. p. 9)

7) In the work of criminal reformation, it is vital to keep in mind that the criminal—not society, capitalism, or the criminal justice system—is the problem.

Some criminal justice advocates take the position that among the people connected with the carceral world, the good guys are the criminals and the police, district attorneys, prison guards, and the legislators who support stringent criminal sanctions, are the bad guys.

This is the absolutely wrong position, for in virtually any carceral population in America it is the criminals who are the indisputable bad guys, while the good guys are the ones protecting the public from the depredations of criminals. Those who parlay the myths of Hollywood or Marxism into an intellectual stance that fails to understand this basic fact, does everyone a disservice—in particular the penitential criminal—who may find little reason for proper expiation within a culture defining criminality as somehow admirable.

Conclusion

Like many fields, criminal justice often benefits from or is hurt by ideas that take hold of an influential group able to create foundational ideology from which taboos against opposing ideas can be created; but in the midst of these philosophical and sociological meanderings, the conclusions from the seminal thinker in current crime and public policy remain valid:

> Rehabilitation has not yet been shown to be a promising method for dealing with serious offenders, broad-gauge investments in social progress have little near-term effect on crime rates, punishment is not an unworthy objective for the criminal justice system of a free and liberal society to pursue, the evidence supports (though cannot conclusively prove) the view that deterrence and incapacitation work, and new crime-control techniques ought to be tried in a frankly experimental manner with a heavy emphasis on objective evaluation.
>
> **—James Q. Wilson (1975)** *Thinking About Crime* **(Rev. Ed. 1983) p. 5—**

References

Amerio, R. (1996). *Iota Unum: A study of changes in the Catholic Church in the XXth Century.* Kansas City; Sarto House

Aquinas, T. St. (1920). *Summa Theologica.* Retrieved March 8, 2008 from http://www.newadvent.org/summa/

Aries, P. & Duby, G. (Eds.). (1987). *A history of private life: 1. From Pagan Rome to Byzantium.* Cambridge, Massachusetts: Harvard University Press.

Belloc, H. (1991). *The great heresies.* Rockford, Illinois: Tan Books

Budziszewski, J. (2004). Categorical Pardon: On the argument for abolishing capital punishment. In E.C. Owens, J.D. Carlson & E.P. Elshtain (Eds.). *Religion and the death penalty,* (pp. 109-122). Cambridge, England: Eerdmans Publishing.

Bureau of Justice Statistics. (2006). *Sourcebook of criminal justice statistics online.* Retrieved April 14, 2008 from http://www.albany.edu/sourcebook/pdf/t67920 06.pdf

Bykowicz, J. (March 9, 2008). Reigning from behind bars, *Baltimore Sun.* Retrieved March 9, 2008 from http://www.baltimoresun.com/news/local/crim e/bal-te.md.willock09mar09,0,464792.story

Canon Law Society of America. (1983). *Code of Canon Law.* Washington, DC; Libreria Editrice Vaticana.

Charles, Rodger S.J.. (1998). *Christian social witness and teaching: The Catholic tradition from Genesis to Centesimus Annus* (Vols. 1-2). Herefordshire, England: Gracewing Fowler Wright Books.

Cromartie, M. (1997). *Buckley on Belief,* Books & Culture. Retrieved February 29, 2008 from http://www.eppc.org/publications/pubID.85/pub_detail.asp

Dulles, A. (Cardinal). (April, 2001). Catholicism & Capital Punishment, *First Things* Retrieved March 8, 2008 from http://www.firstthings.com/article.php3?id_article=2175

Dulles, A. Cardinal. (2004). Catholic teaching on the Death penalty. In E.C. Owens, J.D. Carlson & E.P. Elshtain (Eds.). *Religion and the death penalty,* (pp. 23-30). Cambridge, England: Eerdmans Publishing.

Dulles, A. Cardinal. (2007). *Magisterium: Teacher and guardian of the faith.* Naples, Florida: Sapientia Press.

Dunklin, R. (2009, March 31). Leader of Catholic order that once treated priests like Dallas' Rudolph Kos spoke out in the 1950's. *The Dallas Morning News,* Retrieved May 6, 2009 from http://www.dallasnews.com/sharedcontent/dws/dn/latestnews/stories/033009dnmetpriestpapers.3bcdc77.html

Ertelt, S. (2009, February 16). *Pro-Abortion House Speaker Pelosi will meet with Pope Benedict,* Lifenews.com, Retrieved April 14, 2009 from http://www.lifenews.com/int1086.html

Fenton, J. (2009, April 17). Indictments reveal prison crime world. *Baltimore Sun.* Retrieved April 17, 2009 from http://www.baltimoresun.com/news/local/crime/bal-te.md.ci.gang17apr17,0,4639477.story

Flannery, K. L. (2007). Capital punishment and the law, *Ave Maria Law Review, 5,* 399-428

Glendon, M.A. (2001). A world made new: Eleanor Roosevelt and the universal declaration of human rights. New York: Random House.

Gregory the Great. *The book of pastoral rule of Saint Gregory the Great Roma Pontiff to John, bishop of the city of Ravenna*. Retrieved July 8, 2009 from http://www.clerus.org/bibliaclerusonline/en/index.htm

Hardin, J.S. (1981). *The Catholic catechism: A contemporary catechism of the teachings of the Catholic Church*. New York: Image Books.

Hardin, J. S. (1999). *Modern Catholic Dictionary*. Bardstown, Kentucky: Inter Mirifica.

Haydock, G. L. (1859). *Haydock's Catholic bible commentary, 1859 edition*. Retrieved March 22, 2008 from http://haydock1859.tripod.com/id36.html

Hendershott, A. (2006). *The politics of abortion*. New York: Encounter Books.

Henry, M. (1706). Complete commentary on the whole bible. Retrieved May 6, 2008 from http://bible.crosswalk.com/Commentaries/MatthewHenryComplete/mhc-com.cgi?book=mt&chapter=018

Hollenbach, D. (2008). 'Economic justice for all' twenty years later. *Journal of Catholic Social Thought. 5,* 315-321.

Holy See. (1992) *Catechism of the Catholic Church* Rome 1ˢᵗ Ed.): Libreria Editrice Vaticana, San Francisco: Ignatius Press.

Holy See. (1997) *Catechism of the Catholic Church* (2ⁿᵈ Ed.) Rome: Libreria Editrice Vaticana. http://www.vatican.va/archive/ENG0015/_INDEX.HTM

Hunt, S. (2007) Criminology. In Coulter, M. L., Krason, S. M.,Myers, R. S., & Varacalli, J. A. (Eds.). *Encyclopedia of Catholic social thought, social science, and social policy*, Volume 1 & 2. Lanham, Maryland; The Scarecrow Press, Inc.

Kane, D. (December 5, 2008) Cell phones plague prisons: A smuggled phone can fetch $500, *The News & Observer*. Retrieved December 5, 2008 from http://www.newsobserver.com/news/story/132 1262.html

Krause, E. (2007). Pope Pius XII (1876-1958). In Coulter, M. L., Krason, S. M.,Myers, R. S., & Varacalli, J. A. (Eds*.). Encyclopedia of Catholic social thought, social science, and social policy*, Volume 1 & 2. Lanham, Maryland; The Scarecrow Press, Inc.

Lawler, P. F. (2008). *The faithful departed: The collapse of Boston's Catholic culture.* New York: Encounter Books.

Lawler, P.F. (February 2008). A shrewd move: *Catholic World Report*. Retrieved March 5, 2008 from http://www.ignatius.com/Magazines/CWR/lawl er_feb08.htm

Long, S. A. (1999). Evangelium Vitae, St. Thomas Aquinas, and the death penalty. *The Thomist, 63*:511-552.

Magister, S. (2009). *"According to the scriptures." How to Read the mostly widely read book in the world.* Retrieved May 3, 2009 from http://chiesa.espresso.repubblica.it/articolo/13 38254?eng=y

Montgomery, M. (n.d.). Locked down: Gangs in the supermax, *American RadioWorks*, Retrieved July 8, 2009 from http://americanradioworks.publicradio.org/feat ures/prisongangs/a1.html

Navarre Theology Faculty. (1988). *The Navarre bible: Saint Matthew's gospel.* Dublin, Ireland: Four Courts Press.

Neuhaus, R.J. (October 1995). The Public Square; *First*

Things: A Journal of Religion ,Culture & Public Life. (Retrieved May 20, 2008 from http://www.firstthings.com/article.php3?id_art icle=4086

Newport, F. (2009, March 30). *Catholics similar to mainstream on abortion, stem cells.* Retrieved April 22, 2009 from http://www.gallup.com/poll/117154/Catholics-Similar-Mainstream-Abortion-Stem-Cells.aspx

Pontifical Council for Justice and Peace. (2004). *Compendium of the social doctrine of the Church.* Vatican City: Libreria Editrice Vaticana.

Pope Benedict XVI (2008, April 18) Meeting with the Members of the General Assembly of the United Nations Organization. *Address of His Holiness Benedict XVI.* New York. Friday, 18 April 2008. Retrieved April 26, 2008 from http://www.vatican.va/holy_father/benedict_xv i/speeches/2008/april/documents/hf_ben-xvi_spe_20080418_un-visit_en.html

Pope Benedict XVI. (2008, November 8). The heritage of the magisterium of Pius XII and the Second Vatican Council. Speech, Retrieved March 31, 2009 from http://www.vatican.va/holy_father/benedict_xv i/speeches/2008/november/documents/hf_ben -xvi_spe_20081108_congresso-pioxii_en.html

Pope John Paul II. (1993). *Veritatis Splendor* , Encyclical Letter of John Paul II. Boston; Pauline Books & Media

Pope John Paul II. (1999) Homily. St. Louis, January 27, 1999. Retrieved May 8, 2008 From http://www.vatican.va/holy_father/john_paul_ ii/travels/documents/hf_jp-ii_hom_27011999_stlouis_en.html

Pope Pius XII. (1957). *The Pope speaks: The teachings of Pope Pius XII.* New York: Pantheon.
114

Pope Pius XII. (1961). *The major addresses of Pope Pius XII. Volume 1: Selected addresses.* Yzermans, V. A. (Ed.). St. Paul. North Central Publishing Company.

Ratzinger, J. Cardinal with Vittorio Messori. (1985). *The Ratzinger report: An exclusive interview on the state of the Church.* San Francisco: Ignatius Press.

Ratzinger, J. Cardinal. (1997). *Gospel, Catechesis, Catechism: Sidelights on the Catechism of the Catholic Church.* San Francisco: Ignatius Press.

Rice, C E. (2007). Death Penalty, In Coulter, M. L., Krason, S. M.,Myers, R. S., & Varacalli, J. A. (Eds.*). Encyclopedia of Catholic social thought, social science, and social policy*, Volume 1 & 2. Lanham, Maryland; The Scarecrow Press, Inc.

Roman Catechism (1566). (1982 Edition). *The Catechism of the Council of Trent*: *Ordered by the Council of Trent, Edited under St. Charles Borromeo, Published by decree of Pope St. Pius V.*. (McHugh, J.A. & Callan, C.J., Trans.) Rockford, Illinois: Tan Books and Publishers Inc.

Saint Augustine. (426 A.D.). (1991 Edition). *The City of God.* (Dodd, M.), Trans) New York: Modern Library.

Siegmund, J. M. (2007). Hardon, John A., SJ (1914-2000) In Coulter, M. L., Krason, S. M., Myers, R. S., & Varacalli, J. A. (Eds.*). Encyclopedia of Catholic social thought, social science, and social policy*, Volume 1 & 2. Lanham, Maryland: The Scarecrow Press, Inc.

Skotnicki, A. (Winter/Spring 2002). The U.S. Catholic Bishops on Crime and Criminal Justice; *Josephinum Journal of Theology.* 9(1), 146-157.

Scalia, A. (2002, May) God's justice and ours. *First*

Things. Retrieved May 18, 2008 from http://www.firstthings.com/article.php3?id_article=2022

Stravinkas, P. M.J. (1998). *Our Sunday Visitor's Catholic Encyclopedia,* Revised Edition. Huntington, Indiana: Our Sunday Visitor Publishing.

Thompson, D. (2009, April 14). Prisons press fight against smuggled cell phones. *San Diego Union-Tribune*. Retrieved April 14, 2009 from http://www3.signonsandiego.com/stories/2009/apr/14/california-prisons-cell-phones-041409/?zIndex=82142

Tocqueville, A.D. (2000). *Democracy in America*. (H. Mansfield & D. Winthrop, Trans.) Chicago & London: University of Chicago Press. Original work published in 1835, Vol. 1 & 1840, Vol.2)

United Nations Report. (2001). *The responsibility to protect*. Ottawa, Canada. International Commission on Intervention and State Sovereignty. Retrieved April 22, 2008 from http://www.iciss.ca/pdf/Commission-Report.pdf

University of Navarre. (1988). *The Navarre Bible*. Dublin, Ireland: Four Courts Press.

USCCB. (2005). *A Culture of life & the penalty of death*, *A statement of the United States Conference of Catholic Bishops calling for an end to the use of the death penalty*. Retrieved May 10, 2008 from http://www.usccb.org/sdwp/national/penaltyofdeath.pdf

USCCB, (2006).*United States Catholic Catechism for Adults*. Washington, D.C.: United States Conference of Catholic Bishops.

Ward, M. (2008). Prison officials ask for $66 million to help stop cell phone smuggling, *Austin American-Statesman,* December 4, 2008.

Retrieved   12/4/08   from
http://www.statesman.com/news/content/news
/stories/local/12/04/1204cellphones.html

Weber, N. (1907). Albigenses. In The Catholic
Encyclopedia. New York: Robert Appleton
Company. Retrieved July 4, 2009 from New
Advent:
http://www.newadvent.org/cathen/01267e.htm

Weber, N. (1912). Waldenses. In The Catholic
Encyclopedia. New York: Robert Appleton
Company. Retrieved July 4, 2009 from New
Advent:
http://www.newadvent.org/cathen/15527b.htm

Weigel, G. (1999). *Witness to hope: The biography of
Pope John Paul II.* New York: HarperCollins
Publishers.

Willis, J. (1911). Capital Punishment. In The Catholic
Encyclopedia. New York: Robert Appleton
Company. Retrieved July 4, 2009 from New
Advent:
http://www.newadvent.org/cathen/12565a.htm

Witte, B. (July 15, 2009). Officials ask help controlling
prison cell phones. *Washington Post.* Retrieved
July 21 from
http://www.washingtonpost.com/wp-
dyn/content/article/2009/07/15/AR200907150
1705.html

Wuerl, Archbishop Donald W. (May 5, 2008)
Reflections again on Faith and Public Life.
Retrieved   May   5,   2008   from
http://www.catholicstandard.com/main.asp?Se
ctionID=14&SubSectionID=79&ArticleID=1684
&TM=73887.83

About The Lampstand Foundation

The Lampstand Foundation is a 501 c (3) nonprofit corporation founded by David H. Lukenbill in Sacramento, California in 2003 as a lay apostolate grounded in the social teaching of the Catholic Church, to provide deep knowledge leadership development tools for community organizations— developed and managed by transformed criminals—working to reform criminals.

Mission

Transforming the repentant criminal, suffering from his distance from God, into a deep knowledge leader who can teach other criminals the path to redemption through the social teaching of the Catholic Church.

God longs for the tears of criminals; He thirsts for the tears of sinners.

(St. John Chrysostom)

About the Author

David H. Lukenbill was a criminal—thief and robber—for 20 years, serving 12 of those years in maximum security federal and state prisons. He eventually transformed himself through education, (AA in Criminal Justice—Sacramento City College; BS in Organizational Behavior and Masters in Public Administration—University of San Francisco) many years developing and working with criminal transformative organizations (including founding and directing, for three years, one of the most successful college-based programs for former criminals in California) studying the social teaching, and God's grace discovering and being baptized into the Catholic Church.

He is married to his wife of 26 years and they have one child. They live by the American River in California with two cats, and all the wild critters they can feed.

Contact information at the Lampstand Foundation website, www.lampstandfoundation.org

Prayer to St. Dismas

Glorious Saint Dismas, you alone of all the great Penitent Saints were directly canonized by Christ Himself; you were assured of a place in Heaven with Him "*this day*" because of the sincere confession of your sins to Him in the tribunal of Calvary and your true sorrow for them as you hung beside Him in that open confessional; you who by the direct sword thrust of your love and repentance did open the Heart of Jesus in mercy and forgiveness even before the centurion's spear tore it asunder; you whose face was closer to that of Jesus in His last agony, to offer Him a word of comfort, closer even than that of His Beloved Mother, Mary; you who knew so well how to pray, teach me the words to say to Him to gain pardon and the grace of perseverance; and you who are so close to Him now in Heaven, as you were during His last moments on earth, pray to Him for me that I shall never again desert Him, but that at the close of my life I may hear from Him the words He addressed to you: "This day thou shalt be with Me in Paradise." Amen.

Prayer to St. Michael for Protection of the Catholic Church and Her Members

✠ Glorious St. Michael, Guardian and Defender of the Church of Jesus Christ, come to the assistance of the Church, against which the powers of Hell are unchained. Guard with thy special care her august visible head, and obtain for him and for us that the hour of triumph may speedily arrive.

✠ Glorious Archangel St. Michael, watch over us during life, defend us against the assaults of the demon, assist us especially at the hour of death, obtain for us a favorable judgment and the happiness of bcholding God face to face for endless ages. Amen.

www.ingramcontent.com/pod-product-compliance
Lightning Source LLC
Chambersburg PA
CBHW072234290326
41934CB00008BA/1291

*9 7 8 0 9 7 9 1 6 7 0 7 2 *